ULCERATIVE COLITIS COOKBOOK

Discover How To Relieve The Symptoms Of Ulcerative Colitis With Easy Recipes| 28-Day Meal Plan Included

Kyle Beckwith

TABLE OF CONTENTS

What Is Ulcerative Colitis?

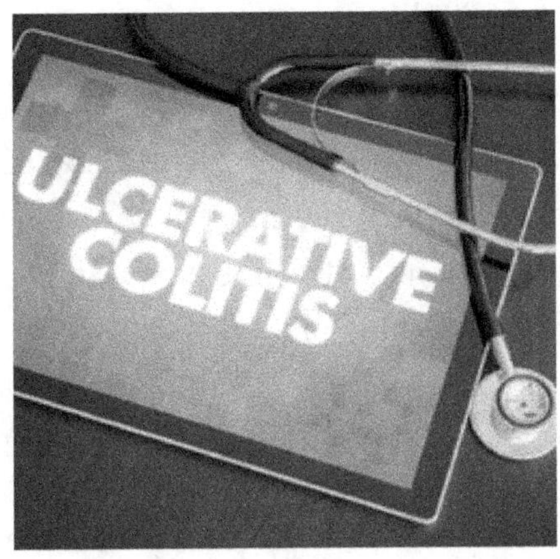

Ulcerative Colitis is a condition caused by an overreacting immune system where it starts fighting your own body.

It starts with your colon lining gets inflamed. If this is not addressed, the inflammation results in little open ulcers and sores on your colon lining.

For some people, ulcerative colitis is a slow and gradual process that starts with inflammation. Unfortunately, we have become accustomed to going for the quick fix instead of digging to find the root of the problem. In this case, many of us opt for over-the-counter medication to provide quick relief from the abdominal pain we start experiencing. This band-aid approach provides minimal relief but then the pain and discomfort persist and we pop more pills until it becomes so bad that we decide to now go for a checkup.

Unfortunately, by this time the disease has already progressed to the point that we now have open ulcers and sores in the colon's lining. Once you have been diagnosed with ulcerative colitis, you will experience seasons of flare-ups and remissions where the painful symptoms disappear.

The goal for you is to stay in a state of remission for as long as possible, ranging from weeks to years depending on the severity of the diseases and the types of treatments you have received.

Well, research has shown that people who are most susceptible to ulcerative colitis include:

- People directly related with someone suffering from any form of Inflammatory Bowel Disease. This could be a parent, child or sibling.

- People between the ages of mid teenage, that is, 15 to 30 years. However, it is important to note that Ulcerative colitis may develop at any age it's just that it is most common between 15–30-year-old.

- People of Jewish descent also seem to have more cases of ulcerative colitis.

What Causes an Ulcerative Colitis?

When it comes to Ulcerative Colitis, doctors and medical researchers have not pinpoint the exact cause of the disease. However, they think the following factors contribute to one having ulcerative colitis.

- An overzealous immune function
- Genetics
- Surroundings
- Gut microbiome

Symptoms You Need to Know

The most common symptoms are:

- Frequent diarrhea
- Very urgent need to pass stool, almost impossible to hold
- Bouts of cramping and pain in the stomach
- Constant urge to pass stool even when you can feel that your stomach is empty
- Rectal bleeding manifesting as blood-stained stool
- Passing pus and, or mucus when passing stool
- Weight loss
- Nausea
- Chronic fatigue
- Fever

People suffering from ulcerative colitis have periods of flare-ups where the symptoms mentioned above manifest and they also have periods of remission when the symptoms disappear completely. Remission can last anywhere from weeks to years.

Low Residue Diet
For Ulcerative Colitis

Ulcerative colitis is a chronic disease that causes inflammation and damage to the colon and rectum. People with ulcerative colitis often have diarrhea and abdominal cramping, and can experience bleeding and pain when the disease flares. People with ulcerative colitis often need to follow a strict low residue diet, which limits the amount of fiber in the diet.

The term "residue" refers to the waste materials that remain after dietary fiber has been extracted from food. In traditional dietary guidelines, fiber is the portion of food that can't be absorbed in the digestive tract and is therefore not used as energy. However, in the low residue diet, dietary fiber is removed and only the waste materials left over after extracted fiber are consumed. This diet is often recommended for people with ulcerative colitis since it limits the amount of fiber in the diet, which often causes diarrhea and abdominal cramping.

Basic Low Residue Principles You Need Follow

One should always follow some basic principles of low residue diet. These are in addition to the foods that should not be consumed during a low residue diet. Let's take a quick look at these principles:

- A low fiber diet must not contain more than 10-15 grams of fiber per day.

- Foods with some fiber like fruits and vegetable must be well cooked.

- Avoid highly seasoned foods. It is not required to completely stop seasoning the food.

- You just need to make sure that the food is seasoned in moderation.

- Avoid eating large meals as they may cause discomfort from gastric distention. Avoid frying completely and try to cook by baking, boiling, broiling, roasting, stewing, microwaving, or creaming.

As far as the length of low residue diet is concerned, it is used temporarily until your digestive processes normalize. Once normalized, you can resume your regular diet, only avoiding foods you cannot normally tolerate.

Foods to Eat & Avoid

Unlike other diet programs, low residue diet offers a wide variety of foods that can be consumed. Let's have a look at these foods and food groups in detail.

Breads and Starches

The following is a list of allowed and not allowed foods for Breads and Starches food group.

Allowed Foods

- White breads
- Muffins Rolls
- Biscuits
- Crackers
- Light rye bread (seedless)
- Pancakes
- Waffles
- Corn flakes
- Rice krispies
- Puffed rice
- White potatoes

- Sweet potatoes (without skin)
- White rice
- Refined Pasta
- Refined cooked cereals

Foods to Avoid

- Whole grain bread and flour
- Granary bread and flour
- Whole grain pasta
- Quinoa
- Pearl barley
- Brown rice
- All cereals that contain whole wheat
- Muesli
- Porridge

Note: Products made with coconut, nuts, bran, seeds or dried fruits are very high in fiber and leave a great amount of residue and hence not recommended in this diet.

Meat and Protein

The following is a list of allowed and not allowed foods for Meat and Protein food group.

Allowed Foods

- Ground, tender or well-cooked lean meats
- Poultry
- Tofu
- Fish

- Eggs
- Creamy peanut butter

Foods to Avoid

- Tough and gristly meat
- Skin and bones of fish
- Pies containing vegetables
- Egg dishes containing vegetables
- Legumes

Vegetables

The following is a list of allowed and not allowed foods for Vegetables food group.

Allowed Foods

- Cucumber
- Green pepper
- Romaine
- Tomatoes
- Onions
- Zucchini Carrots

Foods to Avoid

- Raw high fiber vegetables
- Split peas
- Lentils
- Peas
- Sweet corn
- All seeds

- All pips
- All tough skins
- Potato skins
- Baked beans
- Lima beans
- Green peas
- Broccoli
- Parsnips
- All others
- Juices with pulp or bits

Note: All vegetables are allowed except the ones that are not recommended.

Fruits

The following is a list of allowed and not allowed foods for Fruits food group.

Allowed Foods

- Apricot
- Peach
- Plum
- Honeydew
- Nectarine
- Papaya
- Banana
- Cantaloupe
- Watermelon
- All juices without pulp and strained

Foods to Avoid

- All dried fruits & fruits with seeds Berries

Note: All fruits except those not recommended or those with seeds or skins are allowed

Natural Remedies to Manage Ulcerative Colitis

After years and years of mesalazine, cortisone, and Asacol taken to eradicate the symptoms of ulcerative colitis syndrome, some people find themselves back to square one: sudden discharges of diarrhea sometimes alternating with periods of constipation, bloated belly, cramps, and belly pain. Before we give up, it would be a very good idea to try naturopathy and the many useful and effective remedies and systems to regain intestinal wellbeing and improve or permanently eradicate the symptoms of ulcerative colitis. Finding a natural and permanent solution to attacks of diarrhea, belly pains and meteorism is achievable as long as you do a 360-degree work, going to act on the original causes of the symptomatology. This is possible by touching on the three aspects that in my opinion are indispensable:

- **Nutrition:** by following a dietary program customized according to clinical picture, intolerances and constitution of belonging;

- **Natural supplementation:** taking specific gemmotherapy and probiotics to deinflaminate and soothe intestinal irritation, as well as restore the bacterial flora;

- **Psychosomatic sphere:** almost always, these manifestations result from unresolved inner conflicts. Agitations, worries and anxiety are a great ground for irritating the intestinal walls and establishing an uncontrollable peristalsis mechanism. It is a matter of working with some naturopathic and archeopathic remedies to interrupt this vicious cycle created at the psychic level.

Gut health can be improved through an integrated natural approach that is effective in counteracting the manifestations of ulcerative colitis. Let's look at how lifestyle and natural remedies help the gut perform its functions properly.

TIP #1: LET'S START WITH CHEWING

To reduce the symptoms of our ulcerative colitis, we must first facilitate digestion (which begins in the mouth), and to do this, it is necessary to chew each mouthful of food well and for a long time. Poorly digested foods can trigger inflammatory processes and dysbiosis, which is the colonization of the intestine by harmful microorganisms, to the detriment of good bacterial flora. A useful strategy for getting used to eating slowly is to rest cutlery between bites.

TIP #2: FIBER AND METEORISM

Dietary fiber is essential for improving intestinal transit and counteracting diarrhea and constipation. In addition, fiber also plays an important role in developing new bacterial flora, cholesterol control and prevention from intestinal cancers. So let's ensure that we get the right intake of soluble and insoluble fiber by introducing the right amount between fruits and vegetables, legumes, whole grains dried fruits in every meal. Beware, however, of fiber during an acute phase of intestinal inflammation:

in this case, until the symptoms are in remission, it is necessary to avoid fiber, which could further inflame and irritate the mucous membranes of the colon.

Fresh vegetables are among the healthiest foods: vitamins, minerals, flavonoids and antioxidant pigments in large quantities, plus fiber useful for bowel function and slowing the absorption of sugars and fats, improving blood sugar and cholesterol control.

However, because of the presence of fiber and other compounds that tend to ferment in the digestive tract, vegetables (and some in particular) can cause or worsen abdominal bloating, especially in predisposed people. With these cautions and choosing the right vegetables, you can reduce abdominal bloating and even eliminate it.

First and foremost, it is a matter of favoring certain vegetables with reduced gasogenic effects or even capable of counteracting bloating. Fennel and celery are friendly vegetables for those prone to meteorism because they contain substances that can absorb excess gas that may form in the intestines. Also usually well tolerated by people with irritable bowel are cucumbers, lettuce and zucchini, as well as peppers, carrots and tomatoes.

A second useful strategy is that of gradualness: start by including small amounts of vegetables in your meals, preferring those that least impact the intestines, and increase the quota day by day, contemplating other vegetables in doses that are moderate at first and then more substantial as the discomfort diminishes. Your body will gently get used to accepting an increasingly broad spectrum of vegetables.

TIP #3: PROPER HYDRATION

Proper water intake allows fiber to perform a mechanical action on the walls of the intestine, so that evacuation is normalized and fermentative and putrefactive phenomena linked to intestinal dysbiosis and cause meteorism and abdominal pain are curbed. In addition, stools are softer, thus avoiding problems related to hemorrhoids. The following are the times when it is important to drink water:

- IN THE MORNING (2 glasses): We recommend that you drink a couple of glasses as soon as you wake up; they help activate vital organs and aid the activities of our intestines.

- 30 MINUTES BEFORE MEALS (one glass): A second good time to drink is right before meals, as water will make you feel full and help you eat less. It will also ease digestion.

- 30 MINUTES BEFORE SPORTS ACTIVITY (one glass): This is important to keep your body hydrated and to ensure adequate heart rate control

- AFTER SPORTS ACTIVITY (as much as needed): Water is the best drink for the sportsman (and not only for him) so it is necessary and useful to rehydrate after physical exertion.

- BEFORE GOING TO SLEEP (one glass): A glass of water backs up sleep and allows you to get through the night when the body does not receive fluids for a long time.

TIP #4: PREBIOTICS AND PROBIOTICS FOR LASTING HEALING

From the latest medical research and clinical trials, it is now known and proven that a healthy and balanced gut microbiota is the best way to prevent and treat forms of ulcerative colitis and ulcerative rectocolitis. Periodically promoting the populating of "good" bacteria through the use of prebiotics (substances that provide the necessary nourishment for the beneficial host microorganisms in the gut) and probiotics (commonly known as milk enzymes) is the best strategy we can implement for effective and lasting resolution from any form of colitis.

Even more so, the use of probiotics becomes almost indispensable if one is taking medications that can alter the balance of intestinal flora, such as NSAIDs, cortisone and antibiotics. In this case the necessary bacterial families are enterococcus faecium and sacchharomyces boulardii, resistant to most antibiotics. Among the most interesting prebiotics are inulin and fructooligosaccharides (FOS), while as far as probiotics are concerned, my suggestion for do-ityourself use is to buy formulations containing 5 to 10 billion bacteria per capsule, belonging to different species of lactobacilli and bifidobacteria.

TIP #5: MOVE, MOVE...AND MOVE AGAIN!

Physical activity is a great ally of bowel regularity. If work forces us to our desks for many hours or we don't play sports for any other reason, I strongly recommend you carve out at least 50-60 minutes a day to set aside a brisk walk. This space is as good as a real "cure." Some people find it more enjoyable to walk to the beat of their favorite music, some take the opportunity to explore unfamiliar corners of the place where they live, some appreciate sharing the path with a loved one: anything that helps to create a small, fulfilling daily ritual with movement can be harnessed in favor of intestinal well-being.

TIP #6: LESS STRESS = MORE GUT HEALTH

The gut, rich in nerve cells, communicates directly with the brain. Being able to soothe thoughts and control stress reflexively helps digestive functions. But sometimes irritable colon as ulcerative colitis result from somatization of certain psychoemotional dynamics. By going to resolve and transform these blocks on the inner plane, an unhoped-for resolution can be achieved, permanently.

BREAKFAST

Peach Banana Oatmeal

Preparation time: 10 minutes

Cooking time: 0 minutes

Servings: 2

Ingredients:

- 1 medium banana, peeled and chopped
- ½ cup quick-cooking oats
- ½ cup peach, peeled & diced
- ½ cup plain nonfat Greek yogurt
- 2/3 cup skim milk
- 1 tbsp chia seeds
- ½ tsp vanilla

Directions:

1. Mix the oats, milk, yogurt, chia seeds, and vanilla in a bowl with a lid. Refrigerate for 12 hours.

2. Top with the fruits before serving.

Nutrition: Calories: 282; Fat: 6g; Carbs: 48g; Protein: 10g; Fiber: 2g

Coconut Chia Seed Pudding

Preparation time: 5 minutes + chilling time

Cooking time: 0 minutes

Servings: 2

Ingredients:

- 6 tbsp chia seeds
- 2 cups unsweetened coconut milk

Directions:

1. Mix all the fixings in a bowl, cover, and keep in your fridge overnight before serving.

Nutrition: Calories: 223; Fat: 12g, Carbs: 18g; Protein: 10g; Fiber: 2g

Feta Eggs in Tomato Sauce

Preparation time: 10 minutes

Cooking time: 21 minutes

Servings: 4

Ingredients:

- 4 large eggs
- 2 ½ cups tomatoes, seeded & chopped finely
- 2 oz low-fat feta cheese, crumbled
- 1 tbsp olive oil
- Salt & ground black pepper to taste

Directions:

1. In your large cast iron pan, heat the oil over medium-low heat and cook the tomatoes for 4-6 minutes, stirring frequently.

2. Spread the mixture in an even layer with the spoon. Carefully crack the eggs over the tomato mixture and sprinkle with the feta cheese and black pepper.

3. Cover your pan tightly and cook for 10-15 minutes until the desired doneness of the eggs. Serve hot.

Nutrition: Calories: 178; Fat: 13.2g; Carbs: 5.6g; Protein: 10.3g; Fiber: 1.3g

Vanilla Crepes

Preparation time: 10 minutes

Cooking time: 2 minutes

Servings: 4

Ingredients:

- 4 eggs
- 2 cups refined flour
- 2 tbsp arrowroot powder (if tolerated)
- ½ tsp ground cinnamon
- 1 tsp vanilla extract
- Olive oil cooking spray

Directions:

1. Mix the arrowroot powder, almond flour, and cinnamon in a bowl.

2. In another bowl, beat the eggs plus vanilla extract. Mix both the prepared mixture until well combined.

3. Lightly grease a large non-stick sauté pan with cooking spray and heat over medium-high heat.

4. Pour enough batter and tilt the pan to spread in an even-thin layer. Cook for about 1 minute until the bottom becomes golden brown.

5. Carefully flip the side and cook for about 1 minute more until golden brown. Repeat with the remaining batter, and serve warm.

Nutrition: Calories: 107; Fat: 6.3g; Carbs: 5.3g; Protein: 5.6g; Fiber: 0.5g

Chicken & Zucchini Muffins

Preparation time: 10 minutes
Cooking time: 15 minutes
Servings: 8 muffins

Ingredients:

- 4 eggs
- ¾ cup cooked chicken, shredded
- ¾ cup zucchini, grate
- 1/3 cup refined flour
- ½ cup low-fat Parmesan cheese, shredded
- ¼ cup low-fat cheddar cheese, grated
- ¼ cup olive oil
- ¼ cup water
- 1 tbsp fresh oregano, minced
- 1 tbsp fresh thyme, minced
- ½ tsp. baking powder
- ¼ tsp salt

Directions:

1. Warm your oven to 400°F, and lightly grease 8 muffin tin cups.

2. Whisk the eggs, oil, and water in a bowl until well blended. Add the flour, baking powder, plus salt, and mix well. Add the remaining ingredients and mix until just blended.

3. Place the muffin mixture into the prepared muffin cups evenly. Bake for 13-15 minutes or until tops become golden brown. Let it cool, and serve!

Nutrition: Calories: 164; Fat: 12.6g; Carbs: 4.3g; Protein: 9.9g; Fiber: 1.9g

Pear Pancakes

Preparation time: 10 minutes

Cooking time: 15 minutes

Servings: 4

Ingredients:

- 2 eggs
- 1 cup pear, peeled mashed
- 1 tsp cinnamon
- 2 tsp sugar
- 2 cups refined white flour
- 2 tsp baking powder
- 2 tsp vanilla
- Non-stick cooking spray

Directions:

1. In your bowl, beat the eggs until fluffy. Add the baking powder, cinnamon, vanilla, sugar, flour, and pear, then stir until smooth.

2. Grease your pan using the cooking spray, pour enough batter, and cook until bubbles appear on top.

3. Flip and cook another side until golden. Serve!

Nutrition: Calories: 174, Fat: 2g, Carbs: 3g, Protein: 5g, Fiber: 2g

Strawberry Cashew Chia Pudding

Preparation time: 10 minutes

Cooking time: 0 minutes

Servings: 2

Ingredients:

- 5 tbsp chia seeds
- 3 cups unsweetened cashew milk
- Strawberries, for topping

Directions:

1. Mix the chia seeds and milk in your bowl, cover, and keep in your fridge overnight.

2. Stir in the berries before serving.

Nutrition: Calories: 223; Fat: 12g; Carbs: 18g; Protein: 10g; Fiber: 2g

Breakfast Hash with Sausage & Spinach

Preparation time: 10 minutes

Cooking time: 15 minutes

Servings: 4

Ingredients:

- 1 lb. ground turkey sausage
- 4 small peeled & chopped sweet potatoes
- 2 apples, cored and chopped
- 1 garlic clove, minced
- 10 oz chopped spinach
- Salt & pepper to taste

Directions:

1. Brown the sausage in your pan until no pink remains.

2. Add the remaining ingredients, and cook until the spinach and apples are tender. Season to taste and serve hot.

Nutrition: Calories: 544; Fat: 2g; Carbs: 65g; Protein: 11g; Fiber: 2g

Potato Hash with Egg Scramble

Preparation time: 10 minutes

Cooking time: 25 minutes

Servings: 2

Ingredients:

- 2 eggs, beaten
- 1/2 chopped onion
- 2 cups potatoes, peeled & cubed
- 2 tbsp extra-virgin olive oil
- 1/2 tsp sea salt
- A pinch of freshly ground black pepper

Directions:

1. Heat the olive oil in your large non-stick pan over medium-high heat.

2. Add the onion and sweet potato. Season with salt and black pepper, then cook, stirring regularly, until the potatoes are soft and browned.

3. Transfer the potatoes to your bowls.

4. Adjust the to medium-low heat, and swirl with the remaining olive oil. Add the eggs, cook within 3-4 minutes, and season it with salt.

5. Transfer the egg on top of the potato hash, and serve!

Nutrition: Calories: 320; Fat: 19g; Carbs: 30.3g; Protein: 9.1g; Fiber: 4g

Melon Carrot Protein Porridge

Preparation time: 10 minutes

Cooking time: 8 minutes

Servings: 2

Ingredients:

- 1 cup cantaloupe or honeydew melon, peeled & grated
- 1 small carrot, peeled & grated
- 1 cup milk
- 1 tbsp white flour
- 1 tsp olive oil
- 1 tbsp organic honey
- 1 tsp whey protein powder

Directions:

1. In your saucepan, heat the olive oil and cook the carrot and melon for 2-3 minutes over low heat.

2. Add the milk and honey, and continue to cook over medium heat for 5 minutes, stirring frequently.

3. Mix the white flour with some of the hot milk and add to the mixture. Cook until it thickens a little.

4. Transfer into a bowl, drizzle with more honey, and serve with canned fruits (optional).

Nutrition: Calories: 317; Fat: 6.8g; Carbs: 51g; Protein: 10.9g; Fiber: 1.7g

Breakfast Maple Cornflakes

Preparation time: 10 minutes

Cooking time: 20 minutes

Servings: 2

Ingredients:

- 2 eggs, lightly beaten
- 2 cups nondairy milk
- 1½ cups crushed corn flakes
- 2-4 tbsp maple syrup
- 1 tbsp olive oil
- 1 tsp whey protein
- A pinch of salt & cinnamon

Directions:

1. Warm your oven to 350°F and grease a baking pan.

2. Mix all the dry ingredients in your bowl and spread on the pan.

3. Pour the beaten eggs and milk onto the pan and bake for 20 minutes. Serve warm or chilled, topped with canned fruits if desired.

Nutrition: Calories: 328; Fat: 10.2g; Carbs: 42.4g; Protein: 16.2g; Fiber: 0.7g

Ripe Plantain Bran Muffins

Preparation time: 10 minutes

Cooking time: 18 minutes

Servings: 12 muffins

Ingredients:

- 4 large eggs, lightly beaten
- 2 medium ripe plantains, mashed
- 1 ½ cup refined cereal
- 1 cup refined white flour
- 1 cup of low-fat non-dairy milk
- ¼ cup canola oil
- ½ cup stevia
- 2 tsp baking powder

Directions:

1. Warm the oven to 400°F.

2. In your bowl, combine the bran cereal and milk, and set aside. Add the eggs and oil, then stir in the stevia and plantain.

3. In another bowl, combine the salt, flour, and baking powder. Mix both the prepared mixture until smooth.

4. Pour enough batter evenly into your paper-lined muffin tins, and bake for 18 minutes until golden brown and firm. Let it cool before serving.

Nutrition: Calories: 325; Fat: 19g; Carbs: 37g; Protein: 3g; Fiber: 2g

Potato Omelet

Preparation time: 10 minutes

Cooking time: 15 minutes

Servings: 6

Ingredients:

- ¾ lb. potatoes, peeled & sliced thinly
- 6 eggs
- ½ cup olive oil
- Salt & ground black pepper to taste

Directions:

1. In your large pan, heat the oil over medium-high heat and cook the potatoes with salt and black pepper for about 6-8 minutes, stirring occasionally.

2. Meanwhile, beat the eggs, salt, and black pepper in a bowl. Add the egg mixture into the pan and gently stir to combine.

3. Adjust to low heat and cook for about 2-3 minutes until eggs begin to set. Carefully flip and cook for about 1-2 minutes until eggs are set. Serve hot.

Nutrition: Calories: 246; Fat: 21.2g; Carbs: 9.3g; Protein: 6.5g; Fiber: 1.3g

Banana and Pear Pita Pockets

Preparation time: 10 minutes

Cooking time: 0 minutes

Servings: 1

Ingredients:

- 1/2 small banana, peeled & sliced
- 1 round refined white flour pita bread
- 1/2 small pear, peeled, seedless, cored, cooked & sliced
- 1/4 cup low-fat Cottage cheese

Directions:

1. Combine the banana, pear, and cottage cheese in a small bowl.

2. Slice your pita bread to make a pocket, and fill it with the mixture. Serve.

Nutrition: Calories: 402; Fat: 2g; Carbs: 87g; Protein: 14g; Fiber: 1g

French Toast

Preparation time: 10 minutes

Cooking time: 0 minutes

Servings: 1

Ingredients:

- 2 slices of white bread
- 1 egg
- ¼ cup nondairy milk
- 2 tbsp apple or smooth peanut butter
- 1 tbsp olive oil
- 2 tsp maple syrup
- A pinch of salt & cinnamon

Directions:

1. Mix the milk, egg, salt, and maple syrup in your bowl. Dip both sides of the bread in this mixture.

2. Heat the oil in a frying pan and cook both toasts for 2-3 minutes per side until light brown.

3. Top with apple or smooth peanut butter, and serve!

Nutrition: Calories: 366; Fat: 12.6g; Carbs: 48g; Protein: 11.6g; Fiber: 1.7g

Ricotta Pear Cream Bowl

Preparation time: 10 minutes

Cooking time: 0 minutes

Servings: 4

Ingredients:

- 1 (15-oz.) container part-skim ricotta cheese
- ½ cup canned pears, drained
- 1 tsp fresh lemon juice
- 2-4 drops of liquid stevia

Directions:

1. Place all the ingredients except pears into a food processor and pulse until smooth.

2. Serve immediately.

Nutrition: Calories: 127; Fat: 6.8g; Carbs: 6.8g; Protein: 9.8g; Fiber: 0

Pear And Cornflakes Granola

Preparation time: 15 minutes

Cooking time: 25 minutes

Servings: 2

Ingredients:

- 1 pear, grated largely
- 2 cups cornflakes
- 1 tsp stevia
- 2 tsp olive oil

Directions:

1. Warm the oven to 350°F and grease a baking sheet.

2. Mix the cornflakes and pear in a bowl.

3. In your saucepan, heat the olive oil and sugar until they dissolve. Combine both mixtures and stir to coat well.

4. Spread this mixture onto your baking sheet and bake for 25 minutes until golden brown; stir every 10 minutes. Let it cool, and serve!

Nutrition: Calories: 185; Fat: 6.1g; Carbs: 33.6g; Protein: 2g; Fiber: 2.1g

Cheesy Chicken Spinach Frittata

Preparation time: 10 minutes

Cooking time: 43 minutes

Servings: 8

Ingredients:

- 4 large egg whites
- 2 large eggs
- 4 cups fresh spinach, chopped
- 2 cups cooked chicken, chopped
- 1¼ cup unsweetened almond milk
- 1 cup low-fat cheddar cheese, shredded
- 1 tbsp low-fat Parmesan cheese, shredded
- 1 tsp olive oil
- Salt & ground black pepper to taste

Directions:

1. Warm your oven to 350°F, and grease a 9-inch pie plate.

2. In your pan, heat the oil over medium heat and cook spinach for about 2-3 minutes. Stir in chicken and transfer the mixture into the prepared pie dish evenly.

3. Add the eggs, egg whites, milk, cheddar cheese, salt, and black pepper to a bowl and beat until well combined.

4. Pour the egg mixture over your chicken mixture evenly and top with Parmesan cheese. Bake for 40 minutes until the top becomes golden brown. Let it cool, and serve!

Nutrition: Calories: 158; Fat: 8.3g; Carbs: 2.1g; Protein: 17.5g; Fiber: 0.4g

Spinach Egg Quiche

Preparation time: 10 minutes

Cooking time: 20 minutes

Servings: 4

Ingredients:

- 6 eggs
- ½ cup low-fat milk
- 2 cups fresh baby spinach, chopped
- ¼ cup fresh parsley, chopped
- 1 tbsp fresh chives, minced
- salt & freshly ground black pepper, to taste

Directions:

1. Warm the oven to 400°F, and lightly grease a pie dish.

2. Beat the eggs, milk, salt, and black pepper in a bowl. Set aside.

3. In another bowl, mix the spinach and herbs. Place this mixture evenly and top with the egg mixture.

4. Bake within 20 minutes, let it cool and serve.

Nutrition: Calories: 120; Fat: 7g; Carbs: 4.3g; Protein: 10.1g; Fiber: 0.98g

Apple Cider Cinnamon Waffles

Preparation time: 15 minutes

Cooking time: 10 minutes

Servings: 4

Ingredients:

- 1¼ cup unsweetened almond milk
- 1 cup refined flour
- 3 tbsp water
- 1 tbsp apple cider vinegar
- 1 tbsp ground flaxseed
- 1 tbsp erythritol
- 1¼ tsp baking powder
- 1 tsp baking soda
- ¼ tsp ground cinnamon
- ¼ tsp salt

Directions:

1. In a bowl, mix almond milk vinegar. Set aside for 5 minutes.

2. In a bowl, mix the ground flaxseed and water. Set aside for about 5 minutes until it thickens.

3. Mix the flour, erythritol, cinnamon, baking powder, baking soda, and salt in a separate bowl.

4. In the bowl of flaxseed mixture, add the milk, and vinegar, then stir to combine. Add the flour mixture, then mix until just combined. Set aside for about 5-10 minutes.

5. Preheat the waffle iron and then grease it. Add enough batter and cook for 5 minutes per side until golden brown. Repeat with the remaining mixture, and serve warm.

Nutrition: Calories: 125; Fat: 2.6g; Carbs: 23.2g; Protein: 4.4g; Fiber: 2.4g

Ricotta Protein Pancakes

Preparation time: 10 minutes

Cooking time: 5 minutes

Servings: 4

Ingredients:
- 4 eggs
- ½ cup part-skim ricotta cheese
- ¼ cup unsweetened protein powder
- 2 tbsp olive oil
- ½ tsp baking powder
- ½ tsp liquid stevia
- Pinch of salt

Directions:

1. Add all the fixings except oil and pulse to your blender until well combined.

2. In your pan, heat the oil over medium heat. Add the desired amount of the mixture and spread it evenly.

3. Cook for about 2-3 minutes, flip and cook for 1-2 minutes until golden brown Repeat with the remaining mixture. Serve warm.

Nutrition: Calories: 191; Fat: 14g; Carbs: 2.1g; Protein: 14.4g; Fiber: 0g

LUNCH

Pasta with Cheesy Tomato Sauce

Preparation time: 20 minutes

Cooking time: 55 minutes

Servings: 8

Ingredients:

- 1 large egg, lightly beaten
- 3 cups refined pasta, cooked & drained
- 1¾ cup tomato sauce, divided
- 1½ cup part-skim mozzarella cheese, shredded & divided
- 1 cup low-fat cottage cheese
- ½ tsp dried oregano
- Salt & ground black pepper to taste

Directions:

1. Warm the oven to 375°F, and grease an 8-inch square baking dish.

2. Meanwhile, mix ¾ cup tomato sauce, 1 cup mozzarella cheese, cottage cheese, egg, dried herbs, and black pepper in a large bowl. Add the pasta, and stir well until coated.

3. In the bottom of the prepared baking dish, spread ¼ cup of tomato sauce and top with the pasta mixture, remaining sauce, and mozzarella cheese.

4. Cover and bake for about 45 minutes. Uncover and bake for about 5-10 minutes more. Serve hot.

Nutrition: Calories: 179; Fat: 2.6g; Carbs: 27.5g; Protein: 10.5g; Fiber: 2g

Pasta With Zucchini & Tomatoes

Preparation time: 15 minutes

Cooking time: 20 minutes

Servings: 8

Ingredients:

- 3 tomatoes
- 1 lb. refined pasta
- 1 lb. zucchini, peeled, seeded & sliced
- ¾ cup low-fat feta cheese, crumbled
- ¼ cup olive oil
- 1 tbsp garlic
- 1 tsp dried oregano, crushed
- Salt to taste
- Water, as needed

Directions:

1. Add the tomatoes to your large pan of salted boiling water and cook for about 1 minute. Transfer the tomatoes into your bowl of ice water with your slotted spoon.

2. Add the pasta to the same pan of boiling water and cook for about 8-10 minutes. Drain the pasta well.

3. Meanwhile, peel the blanched tomatoes, remove the seeds, and chop them finely.

4. Heat the oil over medium heat in your large skillet and sauté the zucchini and garlic for about 4-5 minutes.

5. Add the tomatoes and oregano and cook for about 3-4 minutes. Add the pasta and cheese and stir to combine. Serve hot.

Nutrition: Calories: 272; Fat: 10.5g; Carbs: 25.3g; Protein: 9.5g; Fiber: 1.3g

Chicken & Apple Lettuce Wraps

Preparation time: 15 minutes

Cooking time: 0 minutes

Servings: 2-4

Ingredients:

- 1 seedless cucumber, sliced thinly
- 6 oz. cooked chicken breast, cut into strips
- ½ cup apple, peeled, cored & sliced thinly
- 4 large lettuce leaves
- 1 tbsp fresh mint leaves, minced

Directions:

1. In your large bowl, mix all the ingredients except lettuce leaves.

2. Place the lettuce leaves onto serving plates. Place the chicken mixture over each lettuce leaf evenly and serve immediately.

Nutrition: Calories: 165; Fat: 2.9g; Carbs: 8.8g; Protein: 26g; Fiber: 1.7g

Cheesy Chicken Meatballs

Preparation time: 15 minutes

Cooking time: 10 minutes

Servings: 5

Ingredients:

- 1 large egg, beaten
- 1 lb. ground chicken
- ½ cup low-fat Parmesan cheese, grated freshly
- 4 tbsp fresh parsley, chopped
- 2 tbsp olive oil
- Salt & ground black pepper to taste

Directions:

1. Mix all the ingredients except for oil with your hands until well combined in your large bowl. Make small equal-sized balls from the mixture.

2. In a non-stick sauté pan, heat oil over medium heat and cook the meatballs for about 10 minutes, flipping occasionally. Serve hot.

Nutrition: Calories: 262; Fat: 15.3g; Carbs: 0.4g; Protein: 26.9g; Fiber: 0.1g

Beef & Mozzarella Burgers

Preparation time: 15 minutes

Cooking time: 10 minutes

Servings: 2

Ingredients:

- 8 oz lean ground beef
- 1 oz part-skim mozzarella cheese, cubed
- 1 tbsp olive oil
- Salt & ground black pepper to taste

Directions:

1. Add the beef, salt, and black pepper to a bowl and mix until well combined. Make 2 equal-sized patties from the mixture.

2. Place mozzarella cube inside of each patty and cover with the beef.

3. In your frying pan, heat the oil over medium heat and cook the patties for about 3-5 minutes per side. Serve hot.

Nutrition: Calories: 311; Fat: 16.6g; Carbs: 0.5g; Protein: 38.4g; Fiber: 0g

Tuna Stuffed Avocado

Preparation time: 10 minutes

Cooking time: 0 minutes

Servings: 2

Ingredients:

- 1 large avocado, halved and pitted
- 1 (5-oz.) can of water-packed tuna, drained & flaked
- 3 tbsp fat-free plain yogurt
- 2 tbsp fresh lemon juice
- 1 tsp fresh parsley, chopped finely
- Salt & ground black pepper to taste

Directions:

1. Carefully remove about 2-3 tbsp of flesh from each avocado half. Arrange the avocado halves onto a platter and drizzle each with 1 tsp lemon juice.

2. Chop the avocado flesh and transfer it into a bowl. Add the tuna, yogurt, parsley, remaining lemon juice, salt, and black pepper, and stir to combine.

3. Divide the tuna mixture into both avocado halves evenly. Serve immediately.

Nutrition: Calories: 215; Fat: 11.8g; Carbs: 7g; Protein: 20.6g; Fiber: 3.2g

Greek Cucumber Salad

Preparation time: 10 minutes

Cooking time: 0 minutes

Servings: 4

Ingredients:

- 4 medium cucumbers, peeled, seeded, & chopped
- ½ cup nonfat Greek yogurt
- 1½ tbsp fresh dill, chopped
- 1 tbsp fresh lemon juice
- Salt & freshly ground black pepper to taste

Directions:

1. In your large bowl, mix all the ingredients until well combined.

2. Serve immediately.

Nutrition: Calories: 54; Fat: 0.8g; Carbs: 8.6g; Protein: 4.5g; Fiber: 1g

Beef & Spinach Burgers

Preparation time: 15 minutes

Cooking time: 12 minutes

Servings: 4

Ingredients:

- 1 egg, beaten
- 1 lb. lean ground beef
- 1 cup fresh baby spinach leaves, chopped
- ½ cup sun-dried tomatoes, peeled, seeded, and chopped
- ¼ cup low-fat feta cheese, crumbled
- 2 tbsp olive oil

Directions:

1. Add all the fixings except oil to your large bowl and mix until well combined. Make 4 equal-sized patties from the mixture.

2. In a cast-iron pan, heat oil over medium-high heat and cook the patties for about 5-6 minutes per side until the desired doneness. Serve immediately.

Nutrition: Calories: 259; Fat: 17.1g; Carbs: 1.5g; Protein: 25.6g; Fiber: 0.7g

Cucumber Tomato Salad

Preparation time: 10 minutes

Cooking time: 0 minutes

Servings: 5

Ingredients:
- 2 cups cucumbers, peeled, seeded, & chopped
- 2 cups red tomatoes, peeled, seeded, & chopped
- 2 tbsp extra-virgin olive oil
- 2 tbsp fresh lime juice
- Salt, to taste

Directions:

1. In your large serving bowl, add all the ingredients and toss to coat well.

2. Serve immediately.

Nutrition: Calories: 72; Fat: 5.9g; Carbs: 5.1g; Protein: 0.9g; Fiber: 1.1g

European Beet Soup

Preparation time: 10 minutes

Cooking time: 5 minutes

Servings: 3

Ingredients:
- 2 cups beets, trimmed, peeled, & chopped
- 2 cups fat-free yogurt
- 4 tsp fresh lemon juice
- 2 tbsp fresh dill
- 1 tbsp fresh chives, minced
- Salt to taste

Directions:
1. In a high-speed blender, pulse all the ingredients except chives until smooth.

2. Transfer the soup to a pan over medium heat and cook for about 3-5 minutes until heated.

3. Serve immediately with a garnish of chives.

Nutrition: Calories: 122; Fat: 0.2g; Carbs: 14.6g; Protein: 16g; Fiber: 2.6g

Egg & Avocado Endive Wraps

Preparation time: 20 minutes

Cooking time: 0 minutes

Servings: 5

Ingredients:

- 4 organic hard-boiled eggs, peeled & finely chopped
- 4-5 endive bulbs
- 2 cooked turkey bacon slices, chopped
- 1 ripe avocado, peeled, pitted, & chopped
- 1 tbsp freshly squeezed lemon juice
- 1 tbsp fresh parsley, chopped
- 2 tbsp celery stalk, chopped
- Salt & freshly ground black pepper to taste

Directions:

1. In your bowl, mash the avocado and lemon juice until smooth. Add the celery, parsley, eggs, salt, and black pepper. Blend to mix well.

2. Split the endive leaves, and divide the avocado mixture over the endive leaves evenly. Top with bacon and serve immediately.

Nutrition: Calories: 183; Fat: 11.1g; Carbs: 12.7g; Protein: 10.9g; Fiber: 1g

Pasta with Asparagus

Preparation time: 10 minutes

Cooking time: 10 minutes

Servings: 4

Ingredients:

- 1 lb. asparagus, trimmed & cut into 1½-inch pieces
- ½ lb. cooked hot pasta, drained
- 2 tbsp olive oil
- Salt & freshly ground black pepper to taste

Directions:

1. In your large cast-iron skillet, heat the oil over medium heat and cook the asparagus, salt, and black pepper for about 8-10 minutes, stirring occasionally.

2. Place the hot pasta and toss to coat well. Serve immediately.

Nutrition: Calories: 171; Fat: 7.7g; Carbs: 21.1g; Protein: 5.3g; Fiber: 2.9g

Versatile Mac' n Cheese

Preparation time: 15 minutes

Cooking time: 8-9 minutes

Servings: 3

Ingredients:

- 2 cups refined elbow macaroni, cooked & drained
- 1½ lb. butternut squash, peeled, cubed
- 1 cup low-fat Swiss cheese, shredded
- 1/3 cup low-fat milk
- 1 tbsp olive oil
- Salt & freshly ground black pepper to taste

Directions:

1. Cook the squash cubes in a pan of boiling water for about 6 minutes until soft. Drain the squash cubes entirely and return to the same pan.

2. With a masher, mash the squash and place over low heat. Add the cheese and milk and cook for about 2-3 minutes, stirring continuously.

3. Add the macaroni, oil, salt, and black pepper and stir to combine. Remove from the heat and serve hot.

Nutrition: Calories: 322; Fat: 7.7g; Carbs: 44.6g; Protein: 17.3g; Fiber: 1.9g

Roasted Beet Pasta with Kale and Pesto

Preparation time: 15 minutes
Cooking time: 10 minutes
Servings: 3

Ingredients:

For the Pesto:

- 1 large garlic clove, minced
- 3 cups fresh basil leaves
- 1/4 cup organic olive oil
- Salt & freshly ground black pepper to taste

For the Beet Pasta:

- 2 medium beets, trimmed, peeled, & spiralized
- Olive oil cooking spray
- Salt & freshly ground black pepper to taste

For the Kale:

- 2 cups fresh baby kale

Directions:

1. Warm the oven to 425°F, and lightly grease a large baking sheet.

2. In a blender, pulse all the pesto ingredients until smooth. Keep aside.

3. Place the beet pasta on the prepared baking sheet. Drizzle with cooking spray and sprinkle with salt and black pepper. Gently toss to coat well.

4. Roast for around 5-10 minutes until the desired doneness. Transfer the pasta to a large bowl. Add the kale and pesto. Gently, toss to coat well, and serve!

Nutrition: Calories: 288; Fat: 28.8g; Carbs: 7.4g; Protein: 3.1g; Fiber: 2.9g

Veggies and Apple with Orange Sauce

Preparation time: 15 minutes
Cooking time: 16 minutes
Servings: 4

Ingredients:

For the Sauce:

- 2 garlic cloves, minced
- 1 (1 inch) fresh ginger, minced
- 1/2 cup fresh orange juice
- 1 tbsp fresh orange zest, grated finely
- 2 tbsp white wine vinegar
- 2 tbsp coconut aminos
- 1 tbsp red boat fish sauce

For the Veggies and Apple:

- 2 apples, cored & sliced
- 1 cup carrot, peeled & julienned
- 1 cup celery, chopped
- 1 cup onion, chopped
- 1 tbsp extra-virgin olive oil

Directions:

1. In your large bowl, mix all the sauce ingredients. Keep aside.

2. In your large skillet, heat the oil over medium-high heat. Add the carrot and stir fry for about 4-5 minutes.

3. Add the celery and onion, then stir fry for approximately 4-5 minutes. Pour the sauce, stir well, and cook for approximately 2-3 minutes.

4. Stir in apple slices and cook for about 2-3 minutes more. Serve hot.

Nutrition: Calories: 157; Fat: 4g; Carbs: 29.3g; Protein: 2g; Fiber: 3.6g

Turkey Burgers

Preparation time: 15 minutes

Cooking time: 16 minutes

Servings: 5

Ingredients:

- 1 lb. lean ground turkey
- 5 oz low-fat Halloumi cheese, grated
- 2 eggs
- 1 tbsp fresh rosemary, chopped finely
- 1 tbsp fresh parsley, chopped finely
- Salt & ground black pepper to taste

Directions:

1. Warm the grill to medium-high heat, and grease the grill grate.

2. In a large bowl, add all the ingredients and mix until well combined. Make 10 equal-sized patties from the mixture.

3. Place the burgers onto your grill and cook for about 5-8 minutes per side or until done completely.

Nutrition: Calories: 208; Fat: 10.3g; Carbs: 1g; Protein: 28g; Fiber: 0.2g

Shrimp Lettuce Wraps

Preparation time: 10 minutes

Cooking time: 4 minutes

Servings: 6

Ingredients:

- 1½ lb. shrimp, peeled, deveined & chopped
- 12 butter lettuce leaves
- 1 cup carrot, peeled & julienned
- 1 tbsp. extra-virgin olive oil
- Salt & ground black pepper to taste

Directions:

1. In your large pan, heat the oil over medium heat and cook the shrimp with salt and black pepper for about 3-4 minutes. Set aside.

2. Arrange the lettuce leaves onto serving plates. Place the shrimp over lettuce leaves evenly and top with carrot. Serve immediately.

Nutrition: Calories: 164; Fat: 4.3g; Carbs: 3.8g; Protein: 26g; Fiber:0.5g

Fried Rice with Kale

Preparation time: 10 minutes

Cooking time: 12 minutes

Servings: 2

Ingredients:

- 3 sliced scallions
- 1 ½ cup cooked white rice
- 1 cup kale, stemmed & chopped
- 2 tbsp stir-fry sauce
- 1 tbsp extra-virgin olive oil

Directions:

1. Heat the olive oil in your large skillet over medium-high heat. Add the scallions and kale. Cook until the vegetables are tender.

2. Combine the stir-fry sauce and brown rice in a mixing bowl. Cook, stirring regularly, until thoroughly heated. Serve!

Nutrition: Calories: 308; Fat: 11.3g; Carbs: 41.9g; Protein: 9.5g; Fiber: 4.38 g

Shrimp & Tomato Bake

Preparation time: 15 minutes
Cooking time: 27 minutes
Servings: 6

Ingredients:

- 1½ lb. large shrimp, peeled and deveined
- ½ cup homemade chicken broth
- 2 cups tomatoes, peeled, seeded & chopped
- ¼ cup fresh parsley, chopped
- 4 oz low-fat feta cheese, crumbled
- 2 tbsp olive oil
- ¾ tsp dried oregano, crushed

Directions:

1. Preheat your oven to 350ºF.

2. In your sauté pan, heat oil over medium-high heat and cook the shrimp and oregano for about 2 minutes.

3. Stir in the parsley and salt and immediately transfer into a casserole dish evenly.

4. In the same pan, add the broth over medium heat and simmer for about 2-3 minutes until reduced to half. Stir in tomatoes and cook for about 2-3 minutes.

5. Place the tomato mixture over the shrimp mixture evenly and top with cheese.

6. Bake within 15-20 minutes or until the top becomes golden brown. Serve hot.

Nutrition: Calories: 150; Fat: 7g; Carbs: 5.4g; Protein: 25.7g; Fiber: 0.9g

Lemony Scallops

Preparation time: 10 minutes

Cooking time: 5 minutes

Servings: 4

Ingredients:

- 1 lb. sea scallops
- 2 tbsp olive oil
- 2 tbsp fresh rosemary, chopped
- 1 tbsp fresh lemon juice
- ½ tsp lemon zest, grated
- Salt & ground black pepper to taste

Directions:

1. In your medium sauté pan, heat the oil over medium-high heat and sauté the rosemary and lemon zest for about 1 minute.

2. Add the scallops and cook within 2 minutes per side. Stir in lemon juice, salt, and black pepper, and serve hot.

Nutrition: Calories: 166; Fat: 8.1g; Carbs: 3.9g; Protein: 19.2g; Fiber: 0.7g

Chicken Lettuce Wraps

Preparation time: 15 minutes
Cooking time: 10 minutes
Servings: 5

Ingredients:
For Chicken:
- 1¼ lb. ground chicken
- 1 tsp fresh ginger, minced
- 2 tbsp olive oil
- Salt & freshly ground black pepper to taste

For Wraps:
- 10 romaine lettuce leaves
- 1½ cup carrot, peeled & julienned
- 2 tbsp fresh parsley, chopped finely
- 2 tbsp fresh lime juice

Directions:
1. Heat the oil over medium heat in your skillet and sauté the ginger for about 1 minute.

2. Add the ground chicken, salt, and black pepper and cook for about 7-9 minutes, breaking the meat into smaller pieces using your wooden spoon. Remove from the heat and set aside to cool.

3. Arrange the lettuce leaves onto serving plates. Place the cooked chicken over each lettuce leaf and top with carrot and cilantro. Drizzle with lime juice and serve immediately.

Nutrition: Calories: 240; Fat: 15.1g; Carbs: 6.2g; Protein: 20.9g; Fiber: 2.34g

DINNER

Beef Skewers

Preparation time: 10 minutes

Cooking time: 12 minutes

Servings: 5

Ingredients:

- 1½ lb. beef tenderloin, trimmed & cut into 1-inch cubes
- 2 tbsp extra-virgin olive oil
- 2 tbsp fresh lemon juice
- 1 tbsp fresh thyme, chopped
- 1 tbsp fresh oregano, chopped
- 1 tsp lemon zest, grated
- Salt & ground black pepper to taste

Directions:

1. Add all the ingredients except beef cubes to your large bowl and mix until well combined. Add the beef cubes and coat with the mixture generously.

2. Cover and refrigerate to marinate overnight.

3. Preheat the outdoor grill to medium-high heat, and grease the grill grate.

4. Thread the beef cubes onto the pre-soaked bamboo skewers. Place the skewers onto your grill and cook for about 10-12 minutes, flipping every 2-3 minutes. Serve immediately.

Nutrition: Calories: 279; Fat: 5.2g; Carbs: 1g; Protein: 33g; Fiber: 0.2g

Mushroom Goulash with Rice

Preparation time: 10 minutes

Cooking time: 12 minutes

Servings: 2

Ingredients:

- 1 cup mushrooms of choice, halved
- 1 cup cooked white rice
- 1 small yellow pepper, deseeded & finely chopped (if tolerated)
- 1½ cup buttermilk
- ½ cup lettuce, shredded
- 1 tbsp parsley leaves, chopped
- 2-3 tsp olive oil
- 1 tsp mustard
- 1 tsp salt

Directions:

1. Heat the olive oil in your large skillet, and add the mushrooms.

2. Add vegetables, salt, and mustard. Cook within 8 minutes until the mushrooms are well done.

3. Add the buttermilk, and simmer on low heat for 3-4 minutes until the sauce thickens slightly. Stir in parsley leaves. Serve the goulash over cooked rice.

Nutrition: Calories: 276; Fat: 7.1g; Carbs: 40.4g; Protein: 11.1g; Fiber: 1.6g

Mushroom Chicken Platter

Preparation time: 15 minutes
Cooking time: 17 minutes
Servings: 6

Ingredients:

- 4 (4-oz.) chicken breasts, boneless, skinless, cut into small pieces
- 4 cups fresh mushrooms, sliced
- 1 cups chicken bone broth
- 2 tbsp olive oil, divided
- 1 tsp fresh ginger, grated
- Salt & freshly ground black pepper to taste

Directions:

1. Heat 1 tbsp of oil in your large skillet over medium-high heat and stir fry the chicken pieces, salt, and black pepper for about 4-5 minutes until golden brown.

2. With a slotted spoon, transfer the chicken pieces onto a plate.

3. Heat the remaining oil over medium heat in the same skillet and sauté the onion and ginger for about 1 minute.

4. Add the mushrooms and cook for about 6-7 minutes, stirring frequently. Add the cooked chicken and coconut milk and stir fry for about 3-4 minutes.

5. Add in the salt plus black pepper and remove from the heat. Serve hot.

Nutrition: Calories: 200; Fat: 10.4g; Carbs: 1.6g; Protein: 24.8g; Fiber: 0.5g

Easiest Tuna Salad

Preparation time: 15 minutes

Cooking time: 0 minutes

Servings: 4

Ingredients:

For the Dressing:

- 2 tbsp fresh dill, minced
- 2 tbsp olive oil
- 1 tbsp fresh lime juice
- Salt & freshly ground black pepper to taste

For the Salad:

- 2 (6-oz.) cans of water-packed tuna, drained and flaked
- 6 hard-boiled eggs, peeled and sliced
- 1 cup tomato, peeled, seeded, and chopped
- 1 large cucumber, peeled, seeded, and sliced

Directions:

1. Add all the dressing fixings to a bowl and whisk until well blended.

2. In another large serving bowl, add all the ingredients and mix well.

3. Divide the tuna mixture onto serving plates. Drizzle with dressing and serve.

Nutrition: Calories: 277; Fat: 14.5g; Carbs: 5.9g; Protein: 31.2g; Fiber: 0.96g

Prawns with Asparagus

Preparation time: 15 minutes

Cooking time: 13 minutes

Servings: 5

Ingredients:

- 1 lb. prawns, peeled & deveined
- 1 lb. asparagus, trimmed
- 2 tbsp olive oil
- 2 tbsp fresh lemon juice
- 1 tsp fresh ginger, minced
- Salt & freshly ground black pepper to taste

Directions:

1. In a skillet, heat 1 tbsp oil over medium-high heat and cook the prawns with salt and black pepper for about 3-4 minutes.

2. With a slotted spoon, transfer the prawns into a bowl. Set aside.

3. Heat the remaining oil over medium-high heat in the same skillet and cook the asparagus, ginger, salt, and black pepper for about 6-8 minutes, stirring frequently.

4. Stir in the prawns and cook for about 1 minute. Stir in the lemon juice, then serve hot.

Nutrition: Calories: 127; Fat: 6.5g; Carbs: 3.5g; Protein: 14.3g; Fiber: 2.0g

Chicken Salad Sandwiches

Preparation time: 10 minutes

Cooking time: 0 minutes

Servings: 2

Ingredients:

- 4 slices of white bread
- 1 cup chicken, chopped, cooked, and skinless (from 1 rotisserie chicken)
- 2 tbsp anti-inflammatory mayonnaise
- 1 tbsp chopped fresh tarragon leaves
- 1/2 minced red bell pepper (if tolerated)
- 1 tsp Dijon mustard (if tolerated)
- 1/4 tsp sea salt

Directions:

1. Combine the chicken, red bell pepper, mayonnaise, mustard, tarragon, and salt in a medium bowl.

2. Spread on 2 pieces of bread and top them with the remaining bread. Serve!

Nutrition: Calories: 380; Fat: 22g; Carbs: 25.6g; Protein: 19g; Fiber: 3.9g

Brazilian Fish Stew

Preparation time: 10 minutes

Cooking time: 19 minutes

Servings: 4

Ingredients:

- 1 to 1 1/2 lb. of firm white fish
- 1 lime's juice & zest
- ½ tsp salt

For the Sauce:

- 4 garlic cloves, chopped
- 1 onion, diced
- 1 red bell pepper, chopped (if tolerated)
- 1 (14 oz.) can of coconut milk
- 1 1/2 cups of chopped tomatoes, no seeds & peeled
- 1 cup carrot, diced
- 1 cup chicken stock
- ½ cup chopped herbs
- 2 to 3 tbsp olive oil
- 1 tbsp tomato paste
- ½ tsp salt
- 1 tsp ground cumin

Directions:

1. Coat the fish in the 1 tbsp lime juice, zest, and salt.

2. In a pan, sauté the onion and salt for 2 to 3 minutes. Add carrot, garlic, and bell pepper for 4 to 5 minutes.

3. Add the stock, spices, and tomato paste, then simmer for 5 minutes. Add the coconut milk, stir well, and add the fish; cook for 4 to 6 minutes. Serve!

Nutrition: Calories 404; Fat 19.7g; Carbs 12.6g; Protein 44g; Fiber 1.2g

Prawn & Vegetable Pasta

Preparation time: 10 minutes

Cooking time: 30 minutes

Servings: 4

Ingredients:

- 18 medium prawns
- 6 oz of refined pasta, cooked & drained
- 1 large zucchini, peeled, seeded & spiralized
- 2 cups of baby spinach
- 1 1/2 cups of cherry tomatoes, peeled, halved & seeded
- ½ cup of fresh basil, sliced
- 2 minced garlic cloves
- 3 tbsp olive oil
- 1 tsp oregano
- Salt & pepper to taste

Directions:

1. Sauté the oregano, olive oil, and garlic for 1 minute in a pan. Add the tomatoes, and cook for 5 minutes. Add the spinach, then cook until it wilts.

2. In a separate pan, cook the prawns with 1 tbsp oil for 1 to 2 minutes on one side. Turn the heat off.

3. Add the basil, zucchini noodles, pasta, and tomatoes, then toss for 2 minutes. Season it with salt, plus pepper, then serve with prawns.

Nutrition: Calories 246; Fat 5g; Carbs 14g; Protein 10g; Fiber 3g

Turkey with Rosemary

Preparation time: 15 minutes

Cooking time: 10 minutes

Servings: 2

Ingredients:

- 1 lb. boneless, skinless turkey breasts, cut into bite-size pieces
- 2 minced garlic cloves
- 1/2 chopped onion
- 2 tbsp extra-virgin olive oil
- 1 tbsp chopped fresh rosemary leaves
- 1/4 tsp sea salt
- A pinch of freshly ground black pepper

Directions:

1. Heat the olive oil in your non-stick skillet or pan over medium-high heat.

2. Add the onion, rosemary, turkey, salt, and pepper. Cook until the turkey is cooked and the veggies are soft. Add the turkey, and cook for an additional 30 seconds.

Nutrition: Calories: 413; Fat: 17g; Carbs: 6.8g; Protein: 54g; Fiber: 1.6g

Stuffed Zucchini Boats

Preparation time: 15 minutes
Cooking time: 30 minutes
Servings: 3-6

Ingredients:

- 1 lb. ground turkey
- 1 (28 oz) can crush tomatoes
- 6 large zucchinis, divide half lengthwise & scoop out the seeds
- 2 garlic cloves, minced
- 1 small yellow onion, diced
- 4 oz Mozzarella cheese, shredded
- 1 oz Parmesan cheese, freshly grated
- 1/2 tbsp olive oil
- 1/4 tsp garlic powder
- Flat-leaf parsley for garnishing
- Kosher salt & ground black pepper to taste
- Cooking spray

Directions:

1. Warm your oven to 425°F and lightly grease a 9x13-inch baking dish with cooking spray.

2. Brush the zucchini with olive oil, then season with salt, pepper, and garlic powder. Roast in the prepared dish for 20 minutes until it begins to soften.

3. Meanwhile, sauté the onions and garlic in 1/2 tbsp olive oil in a large skillet over medium-high heat.

4. Cook for 3-4 minutes, then add the ground turkey and brown. Add the tomatoes and let them boil.

5. Adjust to medium heat, and simmer until the zucchini is done. Stir in 1/2 tsp salt and pepper to taste.

6. Bake within 5 minutes until the mozzarella cheese has melted. Serve hot, garnished with Parmesan cheese and parsley.

Nutrition: Calories: 173; Fat: 17.1g; Carbs: 10.5g; Protein: 14.2g; Fiber: 3.6g

Roasted Salmon and Asparagus

Preparation time: 10 minutes

Cooking time: 15 minutes

Servings: 2

Ingredients:

- 1 lb. salmon, cut into two fillets
- 1/2 lb. asparagus spears, trimmed
- 1/2 lemon zest and slices
- 1 tbsp extra-virgin olive oil
- 1 tsp sea salt, divided
- 1/8 tsp freshly cracked black pepper

Directions:

1. Warm the oven to 425°F.

2. Season the asparagus with half of the salt and olive oil. Season the salmon with salt and pepper. Spread it on your roasting tray.

3. Add the asparagus on top, and sprinkle it with the lemon zest and slices.

4. Roast for around 15 minutes until the fish is opaque. Serve!

Nutrition: Calories: 507; Fat: 33.8g; Carbs: 4.4g; Protein: 48g; Fiber: 2.1g

Chicken Cutlets

Preparation time: 10 minutes
Cooking time: 5 minutes
Servings: 4

Ingredients:

- 1 lb. chicken breast cutlets
- 1/4 cup refined white flour
- 4 tsp red wine vinegar
- 2 tsp minced garlic cloves
- 2 tsp dried sage leaves
- 2 tsp olive oil
- Salt & pepper to taste

Directions:

1. Place a plastic wrap on the kitchen counter; sprinkle with half the combined sage, garlic, and vinegar.

2. Put the chicken breast on the plastic wrap; sprinkle with the remaining vinegar mixture. Season lightly with pepper and salt.

3. Secure the chicken with the second sheet of plastic wrap. Use a kitchen mallet to pound the breast until it is flattened. Let it stand for 5 minutes.

4. Coat your chicken on both sides with flour.

5. In a skillet, heat the oil over medium heat. Add half of the chicken breast and cook for 1 ½ minute until it is browned on the bottom.

6. Flip and let it cook for 3 minutes. Remove, set aside, and repeat with the remaining cutlets.

Nutrition: Calories: 189; Fat: 5.5g; Carbs: 6.63g; Protein: 26.4g; Fiber: 0.2g

Halibut Curry

Preparation time: 10 minutes

Cooking time: 9 minutes

Servings: 2

Ingredients:

- 1 lb. halibut, skin & bones removed, cut into 1-inch pieces
- 1/2 (14 oz) canned coconut milk
- 2 cups of no-salt-added chicken broth
- 1 tbsp extra-virgin olive oil
- 1 tsp ground turmeric
- 1/8 tsp ground black pepper
- 1 tsp curry powder
- 1/4 tsp sea salt

Directions:

1. Heat the olive oil in your non-stick skillet over medium-high heat.

2. Mix the curry powder and turmeric in a bowl. To bloom the spices, cook for 2 minutes in your skillet, stirring continuously.

3. Stir in the halibut, coconut milk, chicken broth, pepper, and salt. Adjust to medium-low heat and let it simmer. Cook for 6-7 minutes until the fish is opaque. Serve!

Nutrition: Calories: 373; Fat: 31g; Carbs: 5g; Protein: 21.6g; Fiber: 1g

Rosemary Chicken

Preparation time: 15 minutes

Cooking time: 20 minutes

Servings: 2

Ingredients:

- 1 lb. chicken breast tenders
- 1 tbsp chopped fresh rosemary leaves
- 1 tbsp extra-virgin olive oil
- 1/8 tsp ground black pepper
- 1/4 tsp sea salt

Directions:

1. Warm the oven to 425°F.

2. Set the chicken tenders on a baking sheet with a rim. Brush them with oil, and sprinkle them with salt, rosemary, and pepper oil.

3. Bake within 15-20 minutes until the juices run clear. Serve!

Nutrition: Calories: 336; Fat: 13.1g; Carbs: 0.3g; Protein: 51g; Fiber: 0.1g

Lemony Salmon

Preparation time: 10 minutes

Cooking time: 14 minutes

Servings: 4

Ingredients:

- 4 (6-oz.) boneless, skinless salmon fillets
- 1 tbsp fresh lemon zest, grated
- 2 tbsp extra-virgin olive oil
- 2 tbsp fresh lemon juice
- Salt & freshly ground black pepper to taste

Directions:

1. Warm your grill to medium-high heat, and grease the grill grate.

2. In a medium bowl, place all fixings except for salmon fillets and mix well. Add the salmon fillets, then coat them with garlic mixture generously.

3. Place the salmon fillets on your grill and cook for about 6-7 minutes per side. Serve hot.

Nutrition: Calories: 383; Fat: 27g; Carbs: 0.9g; Protein: 34.5g; Fiber: 0.2g

Asian Tofu Stir Fry

Preparation time: 10 minutes

Cooking time: 7 minutes

Servings: 2-3

Ingredients:

- 1 (8 oz) packet rice noodles, cooked
- 1 roasted red bell pepper, deseeded & thinly sliced (if tolerated)
- 1 cup tofu, cubed
- 1 cup canned green beans, halved
- 2 tbsp soy sauce
- 2 tbsp coconut oil
- ¼ cup spring onions greens

Directions:

1. Heat the oil in your saucepan over medium-high heat. Adjust to medium heat and sauté the green parts of the spring onions for 1-2 minutes.

2. Add the vegetables and tofu and stir fry on high heat for 4-5 minutes. Combine the noodles with soy sauce (add more if required). Remove from heat and serve.

Nutrition: Calories: 221; Fat: 6.4g; Carbs: 29.3g; Protein: 11.3g; Fiber: 2.3g

Gingered Turkey Meatballs

Preparation time: 15 minutes

Cooking time: 10 minutes

Servings: 2

Ingredients:

- 1 lb. ground turkey
- 2 tbsp chopped fresh cilantro leaves
- 1/2 tbsp grated fresh ginger
- 1/2 tsp onion powder
- 1/2 tsp garlic powder
- 1/4 tsp sea salt
- 1 tbsp olive oil
- A pinch of freshly ground black pepper

Directions:

1. In a large bowl, combine the turkey, cilantro, ginger, onion powder, garlic powder, pepper, and salt. Make 10 meatballs out of the turkey mixture.

2. Heat the oil in a large non-stick skillet over medium-high heat. Cook for about 10 minutes, rotating the meatballs while they brown. Serve!

Nutrition: Calories: 559; Fat: 47.6g; Carbs: 4.5g; Protein: 28.8g; Fiber: 0.7g

Herbed Salmon

Preparation time: 10 minutes + marinating time

Cooking time: 8 minutes

Servings: 4

Ingredients:

- 4 (4-oz.) salmon fillets
- ¼ cup olive oil
- 2 tbsp fresh lemon juice
- 1 tsp dried oregano, crushed
- 1 tsp dried basil, crushed
- Salt & freshly ground black pepper to taste

Directions:

1. Add all fixings except salmon to a large bowl and mix well. Add the salmon and coat it with marinade generously.

2. Cover and keep in your fridge to marinate for at least 1 hour. Preheat the grill to mediumhigh heat, and grease the grill grate.

3. Place the salmon on your grill and cook for about 4 minutes per side. Serve hot.

Nutrition: Calories: 341; Fat: 27.6g; Carbohydrates: 1.0g; Protein: 23g; Fiber: 0.3g

Grilled Salmon Steaks

Preparation time: 5 minutes

Cooking time: 10 minutes

Servings: 2

Ingredients:

- 1 tsp olive oil
- 2 salmon steaks
- 2 tbsp soy sauce

Directions:

1. Heat the grill, and grease your grill grates.

2. Brush the fish fillets with sauce, and grill for 5 minutes per side. Serve!

Nutrition: Calories 295; Fat 17g; Carbs 7g; Protein 31g; Fiber 0g

Fiesta Chicken Tacos

Preparation time: 10 minutes

Cooking time: 6 minutes

Servings: 8

Ingredients:

- 1 lb. chicken breast, skinless & boneless, cut into thin strips
- 8 well-tolerated corn tortillas, heated
- 1 cup of each sliced red bell pepper & red onion (if tolerated)
- 1 cup mixed salad greens
- 1 tbsp olive oil
- ½ tsp ground cumin
- ¼ tsp salt

Directions:

1. Season the chicken with cumin. Sauté in a pan with hot oil for 3 minutes. Take it out on a plate.

2. Sauté the onion and bell pepper in 1 tsp oil for 3 minutes. Add the chicken back to the pan, and season it with salt.

3. Add the chicken mixture with 2 tbsp mixed greens to each tortilla. Roll to secure and serve.

Nutrition: Calories 320; Fat 6.4g; Carbs 36.1g; Protein 30.3g; Fiber 3.8g

Shrimp Scampi Pizza

Preparation time: 10 minutes

Cooking time: 20 minutes

Servings: 8

Ingredients:
- 1 (13.8 oz) pack of refined pizza dough
- 1 lb. peeled shrimp, cooked & sliced
- 2 cups shredded mozzarella
- 1 tbsp cornmeal
- 1/2 cup ricotta cheese
- 6 cloves of roasted garlic
- 1 tbsp dried basil
- Cooking spray

Directions:
1. Warm the oven to 400°F, and oil spray a baking pan.

2. Stretch the dough over the cornmeal, and place it in the baking pan. Bake for 8 minutes.

3. Mix the ricotta and garlic in a bowl. Spread this mixture on the dough. Add the shrimp, mozzarella, and basil.

4. Bake for 12 minutes, let it cool, and serve!

Nutrition: Calories 175; Fat 5g; Carbs 18.7g; Protein 14g; Fiber 1g

84

SIDES, SALADS & SOUPS

Parmesan Asparagus

Preparation time: 5 minutes

Cooking time: 10 minutes

Servings: 4

Ingredients:

- 1lb. asparagus tips
- 1 cup low-fat Parmesan cheese, grated freshly
- 1 tbsp olive oil
- Salt & ground black pepper to taste

Directions:

1. In your large pan, heat the oil over medium heat and cook the asparagus for 10 minutes.

2. Stir in the parmesan, salt, and black pepper and serve immediately.

Nutrition: Calories: 120; Fat: 9.5g; Carbs: 3.8g; Protein: 5.2g; Fiber: 1.8g

Parmesan Zucchini

Preparation time: 10 minutes

Cooking time: 7 minutes

Servings: 8

Ingredients:

- 6 zucchinis, peeled, seeded & sliced
- ¼ cup low-fat Parmesan cheese, grated
- 3 tbsp olive oil
- Salt & ground black pepper to taste

Directions:

1. In your large pan, heat the oil over medium-high heat and cook the zucchini for about 5-6 minutes.

2. Stir in parmesan, salt, and black pepper, and serve.

Nutrition: Calories: 77; Fat: 6.1g; Carbs: 5g; Protein: 2.4g; Fiber: 1.6g

Creamed Spinach with Tomatoes

Preparation time: 10 minutes

Cooking time: 29 minutes

Servings: 8

Ingredients:

- 20 oz frozen spinach, thawed & drained
- 16 oz cottage cheese, cut into ½-inch cubes
- 2 tomatoes, peeled, seeded & chopped finely
- 1 ½ cup water, divided
- ¼ cup fat-free plain yogurt
- 2 tbsp olive oil
- Salt to taste

Directions:

1. Pulse the spinach, ½ cup of water, and yogurt in a blender until pureed. Transfer the spinach puree into a bowl and set aside.

2. In your large non-stick pan, heat the oil over medium-low heat and cook the tomatoes for about 3-4 minutes, crushing with the back of a spoon.

3. Add the spinach puree and remaining water, then stir to combine. Adjust to medium heat and cook for about 3-5 minutes.

4. Add the cottage cheese cubes and stir to combine. Adjust to low heat and cook for about 10-15 minutes. Serve hot.

Nutrition: Calories: 109; Fat: 5g; Carbs: 7g; Protein: 10.5g; Fiber: 2g

Lemony Green Beans

Preparation time: 10 minutes

Cooking time: 5 minutes

Servings: 4

Ingredients:

- 1 lb. fresh green beans, trimmed
- 1 tbsp olive oil
- 1 tbsp fresh lemon juice
- 1 tsp lemon zest, grated
- Salt & ground black pepper to taste
- Water, as needed

Directions:

1. In a large pan of water, arrange a steamer basket and let it boil. Place the green beans into the steamer basket and steam, covered for about 4-5 minutes.

2. Remove the steamer basket and drain the green beans completely. Transfer the green beans into a bowl with the remaining fixings and toss to coat well. Serve immediately.

Nutrition: Calories: 60; Fat: 3.5g; Carbs: 6g; Protein: 1.5g; Fiber: 2.9g

Citrus Glazed Carrots

Preparation time: 10 minutes

Cooking time: 14 minutes

Servings: 6

Ingredients:

- 1½ lb. carrots, peeled & sliced into ½-inch pieces diagonally
- ½ cup water
- 3 tbsp fresh orange juice
- 2 tbsp olive oil
- Salt, to taste

Directions:

1. Add the carrots, water, oil, and salt to a large skillet over medium heat and let it boil.

2. Adjust to low heat and simmer; cover for about 6 minutes. Add the orange juice and stir to combine.

3. Adjust to high heat and cook uncovered for about 5-8 minutes, tossing frequently. Serve immediately.

Nutrition: Calories: 86; Fat: 5g; Carbs: 10.4g; Protein: 0.9g; Fiber: 2.8g

Braised Asparagus

Preparation time: 5 minutes

Cooking time: 4 minutes

Servings: 2

Ingredients:

- 1 cup asparagus, trimmed
- ½ cup chicken bone broth
- 1 tbsp olive oil
- 1 (½-inch) lemon peel

Directions:

1. In a small pan, add the broth, oil, and lemon peel over medium heat and let it boil.

2. Add the asparagus and cook, covered within 3-4 minutes. Discard the lemon peel and serve.

Nutrition: Calories: 94; Fat: 7.8g; Carbs: 3.9g; Protein: 3.7g; Fiber: 2.2g

Baked Butternut Squash

Preparation time: 10 minutes

Cooking time: 45 minutes

Servings: 6

Ingredients:

- 5 cups butternut squash, peeled, seeded & cubed
- 2 tbsp olive oil
- Salt to taste

Directions:

1. Warm your oven to 425°F, and arrange the foil into 2 baking sheets.

2. In a large bowl, add all the fixings and toss to coat well.

3. Arrange the squash pieces onto the prepared baking sheets in one layer. Roast for about 40-45 minutes. Serve hot.

Nutrition: Calories: 93; Fat: 4.8g; Carbs: 13.6g; Protein: 1.2g; Fiber: 2.3g

Spinach In Yogurt Sauce

Preparation time: 10 minutes

Cooking time: 7 minutes

Servings: 4

Ingredients:

- 2 (10-oz.) packages of frozen spinach, thawed & squeezed dry
- ½ cup fat-free plain yogurt
- 2 tbsp olive oil
- 1 tsp fresh lemon juice
- Salt & ground black pepper to taste

Directions:

1. In your pan, heat the oil over medium heat and cook the spinach for about 1-2 minutes. Stir in yogurt and cook for about 3-5 minutes.

2. Stir in the salt, black pepper, and lemon juice and remove from heat. Serve immediately.

Nutrition: Calories: 85; Fat: 6.1g; Carbs: 5.8g; Protein: 4.3g; Fiber: 2.3g

Cucumber Peach Salad

Preparation time: 30 minutes

Cooking time: 0 minutes

Servings: 4

Ingredients:

- 2 large avocados, pitted & diced
- 1 peach, peeled, pitted & diced
- 1 gala pear, peeled, cored & diced
- 1 English cucumber, peeled, seeded & chopped
- 1 cup cantaloupe, peeled, seeded & chopped
- 1 shallot, chopped finely (if tolerated)
- ¼ cup fresh lime juice
- ¼ cup fresh mint, chopped
- 2 Large lettuce leaves

Directions:

1. In a medium bowl, combine all the fixings except the lettuce leaves. Sprinkle the mint and lime juice, then toss until combined.

2. Let the salad sit within 10 to 20 minutes. Serve over 2 leaves of lettuce per serving.

Nutrition: Calories: 182; Fat: 11g; Carbs: 23g; Protein: 6g; Fiber: 0.4g

Sweet Poppy Seed Salad

Preparation time: 10 minutes

Cooking time: 0 minutes

Servings: 6

Ingredients:

- 1/3 cup distilled white vinegar
- ½ cup olive oil
- ¼ cup maple syrup
- ¼ cup pumpkin puree
- 1/8 tsp salt
- ½ tsp minced garlic
- 2 tsp poppy seeds
- 1 lb. lettuce of choice

Directions:

1. In a blender, combine the vinegar, maple syrup, salt, garlic, oil, and pumpkin until thoroughly combined. Stir in the poppy seeds.

2. Drizzle the dressing over the lettuce, your favorite tossed salad, chopped salad, or chicken salad, and all your favorite fixings.

Nutrition: Calories: 321; Fat: 28g; Carbs: 17g; Protein: 2g; Fiber: 2g;

Watermelon-Tomato Salad

Preparation time: 10 minutes

Cooking time: 0 minutes

Servings: 4

Ingredients:

- 3 cups heirloom tomato wedges, peeled, seeded & sliced
- 3 cups seedless watermelon, cut into 1-inch cubes
- 3 cups trimmed watercress (if tolerated)
- 6 tbsp feta cheese crumbles
- 2 tbsp extra-virgin olive oil
- 2 tbsp chopped fresh basil (if tolerated)
- 1½ tbsp sherry vinegar
- Pinch of salt & ground black pepper

Directions:

1. Whisk the oil, vinegar, salt, plus pepper in your small bowl.

2. In a large bowl, combine the tomatoes, watermelon, watercress, and basil.

3. Pour the dressing over your salad and gently toss to coat. Top with the feta cheese and serve.

Nutrition: Calories: 165; Fat: 11g; Carbs: 17g; Protein: 5g; Fiber: 2g;

Beet Salad

Preparation time: 10 minutes

Cooking time: 0 minutes

Servings: 4

Ingredients:

For the Salad:

- 4 medium beets, scrubbed, roasted, peeled, &sliced
- 4 cups fresh baby spinach (if tolerated)
- 4 oz feta cheese, crumbled

For the Dressing:

- 2 tbsp extra-virgin olive oil
- 1 tbsp balsamic vinegar
- 1 tbsp maple syrup
- Salt & ground black pepper to taste

Directions:

1. Mix all the dressing fixings in a bowl until well blended.

2. Add the beets, spinach, and dressing in a salad bowl, and toss to coat well. Top with feta and serve.

Nutrition: Calories: 129; Fat: 10.2g; Carbs: 7.7g; Protein: 3.2g; Fiber: 1.3g

Cucumber & Tomato Salad

Preparation time: 10 minutes

Cooking time: 0 minutes

Servings: 5

Ingredients:

- 2 cups seedless cucumbers, peeled, seeded & chopped
- 2 cups tomatoes, peeled, seeded & chopped
- 2 tbsp extra-virgin olive oil
- 2 tbsp fresh lime juice Salt to taste

Directions:

1. Add all the fixings to your bowl, and toss until combined.

2. Serve immediately.

Nutrition: Calories: 68; Fat: 5.8g; Carbs: 04.4g; Protein: 0.9g; Fiber: 1.1g

Apple and Mushroom Soup

Preparation time: 5 minutes

Cooking time: 5 minutes

Servings: 2

Ingredients:

- ½ green apple, peeled, cored, & grated
- 3 ½ oz silken tofu, crumbled
- 3 oz pre-cooked refined rice noodles
- 2 mushrooms, sliced
- 1 1/2 cup water
- ¼ cup green chives, chopped
- 1 slice roasted seaweed, crushed

Directions:

1. Add all the fixings except seaweed flakes to a skillet and cook for 1-2 minutes, stirring.

2. Add the seaweed flakes, and serve!

Nutrition: Calories: 366; Fat: 19g; Carbs: 41.1g; Proteins: 11g; Fibers: 3g

Tomato Soup

Preparation time: 10 minutes

Cooking time: 45 minutes

Servings: 4

Ingredients:

- 5 large tomatoes, peeled, seeded & chopped roughly
- 1 carrot, peeled & chopped roughly
- 3½ cups homemade vegetable broth
- ¼ cup fresh basil, chopped
- 1 tbsp olive oil
- Salt & ground black pepper to taste

Directions:

1. In your large soup pan, heat oil over medium heat and cook the carrot for about 4-5 minutes, stirring frequently.

2. Stir in the tomatoes, basil, broth, salt, and black pepper, and let it boil.

3. Adjust to low heat and simmer uncovered for about 30 minutes. Remove the soup pan, and blend the soup until smooth with an immersion blender. Serve hot.

Nutrition: Calories: 122; Fat: 5.2g; Carbs: 13.8g; Protein: 6.7g; Fiber: 2.8g

Beet Soup

Preparation time: 10 minutes

Cooking time: 5 minutes

Servings: 4

Ingredients:

- 2 ¼ cups beets, trimmed, peeled, and chopped
- 2 ¼ cups fat-free plain yogurt
- 2 tbsp fresh dill
- 4 tsp fresh lemon juice
- Salt to taste

Directions:

1. In a high-speed blender, add all ingredients and pulse until smooth.

2. Transfer the soup into a pan over medium heat and cook for about 3-5 minutes or until heated. Serve immediately.

Nutrition: Calories: 87; Fat: 0.4g; Carbs: 15.9g; Protein: 6g; Fiber: 2g

Cantaloupe Gazpacho

Preparation time: 10 minutes + chilling time

Cooking time: 0 minutes

Servings: 4

Ingredients:

- 2 cantaloupes, seeded, peeled, & diced
- 1 English cucumber, peeled, seeded & diced
- 2 shallots, finely chopped
- 1 tbsp apple cider vinegar

Directions:

1. In a food processor, purée the cantaloupes, cucumber, vinegar, and shallots until smooth.

2. Transfer the soup to your container and chill in the refrigerator for about 1 hour. Serve.

Nutrition: Calories: 155; Fat: 1g; Carbs: 37g; Protein: 4g; Fiber: 4g

Shrimp Ginger Soup

Preparation time: 10 minutes

Cooking time: 20 minutes

Servings: 4

Ingredients:

- 1 lb. shrimp, peeled, deveined, & chopped into ¼-inch pieces
- 3 cups low-sodium vegetable stock
- 2 cups shredded kale
- 1 cup full-fat coconut milk
- 1 tbsp olive oil
- 2 tsp minced garlic
- 2 tsp grated fresh ginger
- Sea salt & ground black pepper to taste

Directions:

1. In your large saucepan, heat the olive oil over medium heat. Sauté the garlic and ginger until softened, about 2 minutes.

2. Add the vegetable stock and coconut milk. Let it boil, then add the kale and shrimp.

3. Adjust to low heat and simmer the soup within 5 minutes until the shrimp is almost cooked. Season with salt plus pepper and serve immediately.

Nutrition: Calories: 309; Fat: 19g; Carbs: 9g; Protein: 26g; Fiber: 2g

Miso Whitefish Soup with Chard

Preparation time: 10 minutes

Cooking time: 15 minutes

Servings: 4

Ingredients:

- 1 lb. white fish, thinly sliced
- 6 cups low-sodium vegetable stock
- 2 cups roughly chopped Swiss chard, thoroughly washed
- 2 tbsp white miso paste
- 1 tbsp grated fresh ginger

Directions:

1. Boil the vegetable stock over medium-high heat in your large saucepan. Stir in the miso paste and ginger and simmer for 5 minutes.

2. Add the whitefish and simmer until just cooked through about 5 minutes. Stir in the chard and simmer until wilted, about 3 minutes. Serve immediately.

Nutrition: Calories: 225; Fat: 8g; Carbs: 4g; Protein: 29g; Fiber: 0g

Creamy Carrot Soup

Preparation time: 15 minutes

Cooking time: 35 minutes

Servings: 4

Ingredients:

- 1 tbsp olive oil
- 6 carrots, peeled & finely chopped
- 1 sweet onion, finely chopped
- 6 cups low-sodium vegetable stock
- 2 tsp minced garlic
- ½ cup coconut cream
- Sea salt & ground black pepper to taste

Directions:

1. In your large saucepan, heat the olive oil over medium heat. Add the onion and garlic and sauté until softened, about 3 minutes.

2. Add the carrots and vegetable stock. Let it boil, then adjust to low heat and simmer the soup until the vegetables are soft, about 30 minutes.

3. In a food processor, purée the soup in batches until smooth. Return the puréed soup to the pot and stir in the coconut cream. Season with salt and pepper, and serve.

Nutrition: Calories: 333; Fat: 22g; Carbs: 8g; Protein: 4g; Fiber: 1.3g

Egg Drop Soup

Preparation time: 10 minutes

Cooking time: 11 minutes

Servings: 6

Ingredients:

- 3 eggs
- 6 cups homemade chicken broth, divided
- 1/3 cup fresh lemon juice
- 1 tbsp arrowroot powder (if tolerated)
- Salt & ground white pepper to taste

Directions:

1. Add 5½ cups of broth to a soup pan and boil over high heat. Adjust to medium heat and simmer for about 5 minutes.

2. Meanwhile, in a bowl, add the eggs, arrowroot powder, lemon juice, white pepper, and remaining broth, and beat until well combined.

3. Slowly add the egg mixture to your pan, stirring continuously. Simmer for about 5-6 minutes, stirring continuously. Serve hot.

Nutrition: Calories: 79; Fat: 3.7g; Carbs: 2.7g; Protein: 7.7g; Fiber: 0.1g

SNACKS & APPETIZERS

Cinnamon Peaches & Apple

Preparation time: 10 minutes

Cooking time: 40 minutes

Servings: 6

Ingredients:

- 4 peaches, skin removed & thinly sliced
- 1 lb. apple, peeled, cored & sliced
- 1 cup honey or maple syrup
- 1 tsp cinnamon powder
- 1 tsp vanilla extract

Directions:

1. In a large pot, cook the fruits in boiling water over medium heat until softened.

2. In a large bowl, mix the remaining fixings until well blended.

3. Pour the syrup over fruits and cook until the compote thickens. Pour the compote into a jar. Serve hot or cold.

Nutrition: Calories: 178; Fat: 4g; Carbs: 7g; Protein: 27g; Fiber: 2g

Sweet Potato Chips with Avocado Smash

Preparation time: 10 minutes

Cooking time: 30 minutes

Servings: 8

Ingredients:

- 2 peeled sweet potatoes, cut into thin slices
- 1 avocado, pitted & sliced
- 1/4 cup coriander, chopped
- 1/4 cup lime juice
- 1 tsp sumac
- Salt & pepper to taste
- Cooking spray

Directions:

1. Warm the oven to 400°F, and oil spray 2 baking sheets.

2. Place the sweet potatoes on the prepared tray. Spray the slices, and bake for 20 minutes. Flip, spray with oil, and bake for 10 minutes.

3. In a bowl, smash the avocado with salt, coriander, lime juice, sumac, and pepper. Serve the potato chips with the avocado mix.

Nutrition: Calories 45; Fat 3g; Carbs 14g; Protein 3g; Fiber 2g

Vegetable Fritters

Preparation time: 15 minutes
Cooking time: 3 minutes
Servings: 4

Ingredients:

- 2 large eggs
- 1 large carrot, peeled & spiralized
- 1 zucchini, peeled, seeded & spiralized
- 1 russet potato, peeled & sliced into thin strips
- 1 medium onion, halved & thinly sliced
- ½ cup extra-virgin olive oil
- 2 tsp sea salt
- Freshly ground black pepper to taste

Directions:

1. Mix the carrot, zucchini, potato, and onion in a colander, and sprinkle with the salt. Let the vegetables stand for about 15 minutes. Pat dry with a paper towel.

2. In a separate bowl, whisk the eggs and season with pepper. Mix in the vegetables and stir to coat.

3. Heat a large pan over medium-high heat, and add a splash of oil.

4. Scoop about ¼ cup of the vegetable mixture at a time and form thin patties. Drop them into the hot pan and fry for 2 to 3 minutes, until the fritters are golden brown.

5. Flip and repeat on the other side. Transfer to your paper towel–lined plate, and serve!

Nutrition: Calories: 131; Fat: 12g; Carbs: 5g; Protein: 2g; Fiber: 1g

Applesauce

Preparation time: 10 minutes

Cooking time: 30 minutes

Servings: 4

Ingredients:

- 6 organic apples, peeled, cored, & cubed
- ½ cup boiling water
- ½ tsp cinnamon powder
- 4 tbsp honey
- 2 tbsp fresh lemon juice
- ¼ tsp salt

Directions:

1. In your large pot, cook the apples with boiling water, lemon juice, cinnamon, honey, and salt over medium-low heat until softened. Remove from the heat.

2. Blend this mixture in a blender until well combined. Pour the applesauce into a suitable container or jar. Serve warm or cold.

Nutrition: Calories: 51; Fat: 3g; Carbs: 4g; Protein: 2g; Fiber: 2g

Cinnamon Pear Chips

Preparation time: 10 minutes

Cooking time: 3 hours

Servings: 4

Ingredients:

- 4 pears, peeled, cored & cut into 1/8-inch slices
- 1 tsp ground cinnamon

Directions:

1. Warm the oven to 200°F, and line a baking sheet with parchment paper.

2. Toss the pears with cinnamon in a bowl until well coated.

3. Spread the pears in one layer on the prepared baking sheet. Cook for 2 to 3 hours until the pears are dry. Serve!

Nutrition: Calories: 83; Fat: 0g; Carbs: 19g; Protein: 1g; Fiber: 1g

Avocado Dip

Preparation time: 10 minutes

Cooking time: 0 minutes

Servings: 4

Ingredients:

- 6 avocados, peeled & pitted
- ½ tbsp extra-virgin olive oil
- ¼ cup chopped fresh cilantro
- 2 tbsp fresh lime juice
- 1 tsp fresh lemon juice
- ½ tsp salt

Directions:

1. Mix all the fixings in a bowl until blended and smooth.

2. Serve and enjoy!

Nutrition: Calories: 75; Fat: 1.7g; Carbs: 0.1g; Protein: 13.4g; Fiber: 3.7g

Egg Potato Bites

Preparation time: 10 minutes

Cooking time: 25 minutes

Servings: 12 bites

Ingredients:

- 8 eggs
- 8 oz cooked & peeled potato, chopped
- 1 cup cottage cheese, pureed
- 2 oz Swiss cheese
- Salt, to taste
- Cooking spray

Directions:

1. Warm the oven to 325°F, and oil spray a 12-cup muffin tin.

2. Mix the cottage cheese, potatoes, salt, and eggs in a bowl. Add to the cups, sprinkle with cheese on top, and bake for 30 minutes. Serve!

Nutrition: Calories 90; Fat 4g; Carbs 3g; Protein 8g; Fiber 1g

Potato Sticks

Preparation time: 15 minutes

Cooking time: 10 minutes

Servings: 2

Ingredients:
- 1 large russet potato, peeled & cut into sticks
- 10 curry leaves
- 1 tbsp olive oil
- ¼ tsp ground turmeric
- Salt, to taste

Directions:

1. Arrange 2 baking sheets with parchment paper.

2. In your bowl, add all the fixings and toss to coat well. Transfer the potatoes to your baking sheets in one layer.

3. Bake for 10 minutes in your preheated oven, and serve immediately.

Nutrition: Calories: 187; Fat: 9g; Carbs: 26g; Protein: 14g; Fiber: 1g

Beet Chips

Preparation time: 15 minutes

Cooking time: 20 minutes

Servings: 2

Ingredients:

- 1 beetroot, trimmed, peeled & sliced thinly
- 1 tsp garlic, minced
- 2 tsp olive oil
- Salt, to taste

Directions:

1. Put all the fixing, then toss to coat well in a large bowl. Transfer the mixture to your baking sheet in one layer.

2. Bake within 20 minutes in your preheated oven, flipping once. Serve immediately.

Nutrition: Calories: 80; Fat: 4.5g; Carbs: 6g; Protein: 3g; Fiber: 2g

Homemade Hummus

Preparation time: 10 minutes

Cooking time: 60 minutes

Servings: 4

Ingredients:

- ¼-lb dried chickpeas, soaked in water for a night
- 1 ½ tbsp tahini
- 1 tbsp lemon juice
- 2 tbsp extra-virgin olive oil
- ¼ tsp cumin powder
- ½ tsp salt
- 1 tbsp water

Directions:

1. Cook your chickpeas in a large pot with water over medium heat for about 1 hour. Drain well, and let it cool.

2. Transfer it to your blender with 1 tbsp olive oil, lemon juice, tahini, cumin powder, and salt. Blend until your hummus gets a soft, creamy texture equally.

3. Drizzle with 1 tbsp of extra-virgin olive oil, and serve!

Nutrition: Calories: 207; Fat: 16g; Carbs: 5g; Protein: 12g; Fiber: 1g

Baked Apricots with Honey

Preparation time: 10 minutes

Cooking time: 15 minutes

Servings: 4

Ingredients:

- 4 ripe apricots, halved & pitted
- ¼ cup raw honey
- ¼ tsp ground ginger
- ¼ tsp ground nutmeg
- Cooking spray

Directions:

1. Warm the oven to 400°F and grease a large baking pan with cooking spray.

2. Arrange the apricots in one layer on the prepared pan, and cut the sides up. Drizzle the honey over your apricots, and sprinkle with ginger and nutmeg.

3. Bake within 12 to 15 minutes or until the apricots are tender. Serve!

Nutrition: Calories: 121; Fat: 4g; Carbs: 23g; Protein: 2g; Fiber: 2g

Pear And Apple Crisps

Preparation time: 10 minutes

Cooking time: 30 minutes

Servings: 2

Ingredients:

- 1 large apple, peeled, cored & thinly sliced
- 1 large pear, peeled, cored & thinly sliced
- 1 tbsp olive oil
- 1 tsp cinnamon
- Himalayan salt to taste

Directions:

1. Warm the oven to 410°F and line a baking sheet with foil.

2. Spread the fruits on the baking sheet, drizzle them with oil, and season it with cinnamon.

3. Bake for 30 minutes until tender, let it cool, and serve!

Nutrition: Calories: 108; Fat: 0.1g; Carbs: 14g; Protein: 0.3g; Fiber: 1.4g

Peach And Cream

Preparation time: 10 minutes

Cooking time: 0 minutes

Servings: 2

Ingredients:

- ½ cup fat-free cream
- ¼ cup coconut water
- 1 cup canned peaches
- ½ tbsp honey
- A pinch of Himalayan salt

Directions:

1. Blend the cream, coconut water, honey, and Himalayan salt in your blender until smooth.

2. Serve the mixture in a bowl and top with peaches.

Nutrition: Calories: 108; Fat: 2.1g; Carbs: 24.4g; Protein: 1g; Fiber: 1.3g

Herby Cheese Biscuits

Preparation time: 10 minutes
Cooking time: 15-20 minutes
Servings: 6-8 biscuits

Ingredients:

- 1 cup all-purpose flour
- ¼ tsp salt
- 6 tbsp cold butter
- ¼ cup buttermilk
- ½ tbsp dried parsley
- ½ tbsp baking powder
- ¼ tsp garlic powder
- ½ cup parmesan cheese, grated
- ½ tbsp dried thyme

Directions:

1. Warm the oven to 400°F and line a baking tray with parchment paper.

2. Stir the flour, salt, baking powder, and garlic powder in a bowl. Add cold butter, and mix to form a coarse dough.

3. Add the cheese and herbs, mix well, then slowly add the buttermilk. Combine to form a moist dough, neither sticky nor dry.

4. Scoop ¼ cup of dough per biscuit into a greased baking tray. Bake for 15-20 minutes, until the sides and bottoms are golden browns.

Nutrition: Calories: 184; Fat: 10.2g; Carbs: 8.3g; Protein: 5g; Fiber: 0.6g

Low-Fiber Apple Butter

Preparation time: 10 minutes

Cooking time: 35 minutes

Servings: 1 small jar

Ingredients:

- 2 cups apples, peeled, cored & grated
- 3 tbsp maple syrup
- 1/3 cup water
- 1 tbsp apple cider vinegar
- A pinch of cinnamon
- A pinch of salt

Directions:

1. Add the apples and water to a wide-bottomed pan. Add the salt, maple syrup, and vinegar.

2. Let it boil over high heat. Adjust to a simmer and cook over low heat for 15 minutes. Stir frequently to prevent it from burning.

3. Remove, cool, and blend in your blender to a puree. Cook again over medium heat for 20-25 minutes.

4. Stir well and add a pinch of cinnamon for added flavor. Serve immediately or store in a jar.

Nutrition: Calories: 56; Fat: 0g; Carbs: 9.4g; Protein: 1g; Fiber: 0.5g

Rice Flakes Protein Bar

Preparation time: 10 minutes + chilling time

Cooking time: 0 minutes

Servings: 8-10 bars

Ingredients:

- ¾ cup smooth peanut butter
- 2 tbsp maple syrup
- ¼ cup canned nectarines, finely chopped
- ¼ cup protein powder
- ½ cup toasted rice or corn flakes
- ¼ tsp salt

Directions:

1. Toast the rice flakes in a frying pan over low heat for 5 minutes. Set aside to cool.

2. Crush the flakes and combine them with other ingredients in a bowl. Mix well to form a dough.

3. Smooth into a 4 x 4 pan lined with parchment paper. Let it set in the fridge for 2-3 hours. Remove and cut into bars, and serve!

Nutrition: Calories: 128; Fat: 5.3g; Carbs: 15.6g; Protein: 4.7g; Fiber: 1g

Sweet Dill Dip

Preparation time: 10 minutes

Cooking time: 0 minutes

Servings: ½ cup

Ingredients:

- ½ cup organic plain yogurt
- A handful of fresh dill leaves, finely chopped
- 1 tsp honey

Directions:

1. Blend all the fixings in your blender until smooth.

2. Serve with peeled fruit and crackers or use as a dip with whatever you fancy.

Nutrition: Calories: 25; Fat: 1g; Carbs: 3g; Protein: 1.2g; Fiber: 0g

DESSERTS

Strawberry Gummies

Preparation time: 5 minutes + cooling time

Cooking time: 20 minutes

Servings: 4

Ingredients:

- 1 cup strawberries, hulled, chopped
- ¾ cup water
- 2 tbsp gelatin

Directions:

1. Boil the water and berries in a saucepan over high heat. Remove from heat as soon as the mixture begins to boil.

2. Transfer to your blender, then blend until smooth. Add the gelatin, then blend once more.

1. Pour your mixture into a gummy silicone mold.

2. Place on a tray in your refrigerator to set for about 4 hours. Serve!

Nutrition: Calories: 24; Fat: 0.1g; Carbs: 2.9g; Protein: 3.2g; Fiber: 0.7g

Fruity Jell-O Stars

Preparation time: 15 minutes + cooling time

Cooking time: 0 minutes

Servings: 4

Ingredients:

- 1 tbsp gelatin, powdered
- ¾ cup boiling water
- 3 ½ cups canned fruit
- 1 tbsp honey
- 1 tsp lemon juice

Directions:

1. Blend all the fixings except the gelatin in your blender. Add the gelatin, then blend once more.

2. Pour your mixture into a gummy silicone mold. Place on your tray in the refrigerator to set for about 4 hours. Serve!

Nutrition: Calories: 50; Fat: 0g; Carbs: 11.8g; Protein: 1.8g; Fiber: 0.9g

Cranberry Kombucha Jell-O

Preparation time: 5 minutes + chilling time

Cooking time: 0 minutes

Servings: 6

Ingredients:

- ¼ cup water, at room temperature
- ¼ cup hot water
- 1 tbsp gelatin
- 1 cup unsweetened cranberry kombucha

Directions:

1. Combine the gelatin and room temperature water in your bowl, stirring until fully dissolved.

2. Stir in hot water, then leave it to rest for about 2 minutes. Add in the kombucha and stir until combined.

3. Transfer to your containers, then place on a tray in the refrigerator to set for about 4 hours. Serve!

Nutrition: Calories: 15; Fat: 0g; Carbs: 0.9g; Protein: 0g; Fiber: 0g

Apple Cider Muffins

Preparation time: 15 minutes
Cooking time: 14 minutes
Servings: 12 muffins

Ingredients:

- 2 cups all-purpose flour
- ½ cup stevia
- 1 tsp baking soda
- 1 tsp baking powder
- 1 tsp pumpkin pie spice
- ¼ tsp table salt
- 1 cup apple cider
- 2 tbsp avocado oil
- ¼ cup no-added-sugar applesauce
- ½ cup unsweetened nondairy milk
- 1 tsp pure vanilla extract
- Nonstick cooking spray

Directions:

1. Warm the oven to 350°F, and spray a muffin pan with cooking spray. Set aside.

2. Whisk the flour, stevia, baking soda, baking powder, pumpkin pie spice, and salt in your medium bowl.

3. Mix the apple cider, oil, applesauce, milk, and vanilla in your separate bowl. Combine half of the wet ingredients into the dry, fold to mix, then fold in the remaining wet ingredients.

4. Fill each muffin mold about three-quarters full. Bake within 12 to 14 minutes, until the tops are golden brown. Let it cool for 1 minute in the pan, then cool the muffins on a wire rack.

Nutrition: Calories: 168; Fat: 3g; Carbs: 33g; Protein: 2g; Fiber: 1g

Plum & Nectarine Pudding

Preparation time: 15 minutes + chilling time

Cooking time: 0 minutes

Servings: 5

Ingredients:

- 1 large nectarine, peeled, seeded & sliced
- 2 small plums, peeled & seeded
- 2 tbsp gelatin
- 1 ½ cup water, room temperature
- 2 cups boiling water
- 2 tsp lemon juice
- 1/8 cup honey
- 1 tsp vanilla
- 1/2 tsp sea salt

Directions:

1. Add the fruits, room temperature water, lemon juice, and vanilla to your blender until smooth. Strain through a fine-mesh strainer.

2. Combine the gelatin and fruit mixture, stirring until fully dissolved. Stir in hot water, then leave to rest for about 2 minutes.

3. Add all the remaining fixings and stir until combined.

4. Transfer to your containers, then place on a tray in the refrigerator to set for about 4 hours. Serve!

Nutrition: Calories: 99; Fat: 0.1g; Carbs: 23g; Protein: 2.8g; Fiber: 0.7g

Rice Pudding

Preparation time: 5 minutes

Cooking time: 5 minutes

Servings: 4

Ingredients:

- 1 cup unsweetened nondairy milk
- 2 tbsp pure maple syrup
- 1 tbsp chia seeds
- 1 tsp ground cinnamon
- Pinch of salt
- 2 cups cooked jasmine rice

Directions:

1. In your small pot over medium-high heat, mix the milk, maple syrup, chia seeds, cinnamon, and salt.

2. Bring the mixture to a simmer within 5 minutes, then remove the pot from the heat and stir in the cooked rice. Cover and let it rest for 2 minutes. Serve warm or chilled.
   Nutrition: Calories: 227; Fat: 3g; Carbs: 47g; Protein: 5g; Fiber: 2g

Chocolate English Custard

Preparation time: 10 minutes + chilling time

Cooking time: 10 minutes

Servings: 2

Ingredients:

- 1½ tbsp tapioca starch
- 1 egg
- 1 tbsp pure maple syrup
- ¾ cup almond milk
- 1 tbsp water
- 1½ tbsp cocoa powder

Directions:

1. Add all the fixings to a saucepan and whisk until all lumps are removed. Place the saucepan on the stove and boil over low heat while stirring constantly.

2. Switch off the heat once the mixture thickens. Pour into ramekins and refrigerate for 3 hours before serving.

Nutrition: Calories: 122; Fat: 3.6g; Carbs: 20.5g; Protein: 3.9g; Fiber: 1.6g

Lemon Gelatin

Preparation time: 10 minutes + chilling time

Cooking time: 0 minutes

Servings: 2

Ingredients:

- 3 tbsp powdered gelatin
- 1½ cup stevia
- 1 1/2 cups boiling water
- 3 cups cold water
- 1 1/8 cups lemon juice
- 1/2 tsp lemon zest

Directions:

1. Combine the gelatin and room temperature water, stirring until fully dissolved. Stir in hot water, then leave to rest for about 2 minutes.

2. Add all the remaining fixings and stir until combined.

3. Transfer to your containers, then place on a tray in the refrigerator to set for about 4 hours. Serve!

Nutrition: Calories: 66; Fat: 0.3g; Carbs: 135.6g; Protein: 9.4g; Fiber: 0.4g

Sugar–Free Cinnamon Jelly

Preparation time: 10 minutes + chilling time

Cooking time: 0 minutes

Servings: 2

Ingredients:

- 1 cup hot herbal tea
- 1 cup room temperature water
- 2 tsp gelatin
- 1/3 cup stevia

Directions:

1. Combine your gelatin and room temperature water, stirring until fully dissolved. Stir in the herbal tea, then leave to rest for about 2 minutes.

2. Add the gelatin and stir until combined. Transfer to your containers, then place on a tray in the refrigerator to set for about 4 hours. Serve!

Nutrition: Calories: 113; Fat: 0g; Carbs: 28.4g; Protein: 2.2g; Fiber: 0g

Grapefruit Gelatin

Preparation time: 10 minutes + chilling time

Cooking time: 3-5 minutes

Servings: 4

Ingredients:

- 1 tbsp grass-fed gelatin powder
- 1¼ cup fresh grapefruit juice
- ¾ cup cold water, divided
- ¼ cup raw honey
- pinch of sea salt

Directions:

1. In a bowl, soak the gelatin in ¼ cup of cold water. Set aside.

2. Add the remaining water and honey over medium heat in your small saucepan and let it boil. Simmer for about 3 minutes until honey is dissolved completely.

3. Remove and stir in the soaked gelatin until dissolved completely. Set aside.

4. After cooling, stir in the grapefruit juice and salt. Transfer the mixture into your serving bowls and refrigerate for about 4 hours or until set.

Nutrition: Calories: 94; Fat: 0.1g; Carbs: 23.3g; Protein: 2g; Fiber: 0g

Tangerine Gelatin

Preparation time: 10 minutes

Cooking time: 0 minutes

Servings: 4

Ingredients:

- 1 tbsp Grass-fed tangerine gelatin powder
- 2 ¼ cups Boiling water

Directions:

1. Add the gelatin and boiling water to a large bowl and stir until dissolved completely.

2. Divide into serving bowls and refrigerate until set completely before serving.

Nutrition: Calories: 13; Fat: 0g; Carbs: 0.4g; Protein: 2.8g; Fiber: 0g

Grape Gelatin

Preparation time: 10 minutes + chilling time

Cooking time: 0 minutes

Servings: 8

Ingredients:

- 1 tbsp grass-fed gelatin powder
- ¼ cup hot water
- ¼ cup cold water
- 1 cup fresh grape juice

Directions:

1. In your bowl, soak the gelatin in cold water. Set aside for about 5 minutes.

2. Add the hot water and mix well. Set aside for about 1-2 minutes. Add the grape juice and mix well.

3. Divide into serving bowls and refrigerate until set completely before serving.

Nutrition: Calories: 15; Fat: 0g; Carbs: 2.8g; Protein: 0.9g; Fiber: 0g

Apple Gelatin

Preparation time: 10 minutes + chilling time

Cooking time: 0 minutes

Servings: 6

Ingredients:

- 1 tbsp grass-fed gelatin powder
- ¼ cup boiling water
- 1 ¾ cup warm fresh apple juice
- 1-2 drops of fresh lemon juice

Directions:

1. In a medium bowl, add the gelatin powder. Add just enough warm apple juice to cover the gelatin and stir well.

2. Set aside within 2-3 minutes until it forms a thick syrup. Add the boiling water and stir until gelatin is dissolved completely.

3. Add the remaining apple juice and lemon juice and stir well.

4. Transfer the mixture into a parchment paper-lined baking dish and refrigerate for 2 hours or until the top is firm before serving.

Nutrition: Calories: 37; Fat: 0.1g; Carbs: 8.2g; Protein: 1.1g; Fiber: 0.2g

Peach Gelatin

Preparation time: 10 minutes + chilling time

Cooking time: 5 minutes

Servings: 10

Ingredients:

- 2 tbsp grass-fed gelatin powder
- 2 tbsp honey
- 4 ½ cups fresh peach juice, divided

Directions:

1. In a bowl, soak the gelatin in ½ cup of juice. Set aside for about 5 minutes.

2. In a medium pan, add the remaining juice over medium heat and bring to a gentle boil. Remove and stir in honey.

3. Add your gelatin mixture and stir until dissolved. Transfer the mixture to your large baking dish and refrigerate until set completely before serving.

Nutrition: Calories: 66; Fat: 0g; Carbs: 15.5g; Protein: 1.2g; Fiber: 0g

Cinnamon Gelatin

Preparation time: 10 minutes

Cooking time: 5 minutes

Servings: 2

Ingredients:

- 1 cup of filtered water
- 1 cinnamon stick
- 2 tsp grass-fed gelatin powder
- 2 tbsp honey

Directions:

1. Add the water over medium heat in a small pan and let it boil. Add in the cinnamon stick and turn off the heat.

2. Immediately, cover the pan and steep for 3 minutes. Add the gelatin and beat until well combined.

3. Transfer the mixture to your baking dish and set aside to cool for about 2 hours. Refrigerate to set before serving.

Nutrition: Calories: 76; Fat: 0g; Carbs: 17.3g; Protein: 3.7g; Fiber: 0g

White Chocolate Pudding

Preparation time: 10 minutes

Cooking time: 5-8 minutes

Servings: 2-3

Ingredients:

- 2 tbsp stevia
- A pinch of salt
- 1 large egg
- 2 tbsp tapioca flour
- 1 cup non-dairy milk
- 3 oz unsweetened white chocolate chips

Directions:

1. Mix the dry ingredients in a saucepan. Add the milk and whisk until smooth.

2. Cook mixture over medium heat and frequently stir until thick and bubbly. Adjust to low heat and cook for 2-3 minutes. Remove from heat.

3. Whisk the mixture with egg and add to the saucepan. Let it boil over low heat. Cook and stir within 2 minutes. Add the chocolate chip and stir until melted.

4. Transfer to a bowl, stir well, and let it cool for 15 minutes. Cover with plastic wrap and serve warm or cold.

Nutrition: Calories: 387; Fat: 19.3g; Carbs: 41.5g; Protein: 8.3g; Fiber: 0.5g

Banana And Apricot Ice Cream

Preparation time: 10 minutes + freezing time

Cooking time: 0 minutes

Servings: 2

Ingredients:

- 1 cup ripe banana slices
- ½ cup canned apricot slices
- 1 cup non-dairy milk

Directions:

1. Blend all the fixings in your blender until smooth.

2. Serve immediately or freeze in a silicon container to firm up more — but not overnight.

Nutrition: Calories: 152; Fat: 1.7g; Carbs: 31g; Protein: 5.1g; Fiber: 1.9g

Peach Mango Sorbet

Preparation time: 10 minutes + freezing time

Cooking time: 0 minutes

Servings: 2

Ingredients:

- 1½ cups canned peaches
- 3-4 tbsp stevia
- 1 cup canned mangoes/cherries

Directions:

1. Blend all the fixings in your blender until smooth

2. Transfer to your container, cover, and keep in your freezer overnight.

Nutrition: Calories: 81; Fat: 0.1g; Carbs: 21.3g; Protein: 0.6g; Fiber: 1g

Peach Cherry Jam

Preparation time: 10 minutes

Cooking time: 10 minutes

Servings: 1 cup

Ingredients:

- 2 cups peach, grated
- ½ cup of water
- 1 cup canned cherries
- 1 tbsp honey

Directions:

1. Cook the peach and cherries in a saucepan with water. Simmer within 8-10 minutes until it forms a thick liquid.

2. Add the honey and stir well. Let it cool, store it in your airtight container and keep it in your fridge until ready to serve.

Nutrition: Calories: 53; Fat: 0g; Carbs: 10.4g; Protein: 0.4g; Fiber: 0.5g

Frozen Strawberry-Peach Pops

Preparation time: 10 minutes + freezing time

Cooking time: 10 minutes

Servings: 5

Ingredients:

- 1/2 cup stevia
- 6 oz canned strawberries
- 6 oz canned peaches
- 4 oz water
- 1 tbsp lemon juice

Directions:

1. Boil the water and stevia in your saucepan over medium heat. Allow the mixture to simmer, stirring until the sugar dissolves. Let it cool.

2. Add all the fixings into your blender, and blend until smooth. Set a fine-mesh strainer in a bowl, and strain the juice.

3. Pour your juice into your ice-pop molds, filling every three-quarters of the way. Add in your ice pop sticks, then set to freeze for at least 5 hours or until solid. Serve!

Nutrition: Calories: 99; Fat: 0.1g; Carbs: 25g; Protein: 0.4g; Fiber: 1g

Honey Lemonade Popsicles

Preparation time: 10 minutes + freezing time

Cooking time: 0 minutes

Servings: 2

Ingredients:

- 1/2 cup honey
- 12 oz lemon juice
- 6 oz water

Directions:

1. Mix the honey and water in your saucepan over medium heat. Allow the mixture to simmer, stirring until the honey melts. Let it cool.

2. In a spouted container, combine all your ingredients. Pour your juice into your ice-pop molds, filling every three-quarters of the way.

3. Add in your ice pop sticks, then set to freeze for at least 5 hours or until solid. Serve.

Nutrition: Calories: 292; Fat:0.4g; Carbs: 30.9g; Protein: 0.8g; Fiber: 0.6g

Orange Strawberry Popsicles

Preparation time: 10 minutes + freezing time

Cooking time: 0 minutes

Servings: 12 popsicles

Ingredients:

- 4 cups canned strawberry, hulled
- 2 cups orange juice
- 1 lime, juiced
- 1/4 cup honey

Directions:

1. Blend all the fixings into your blender until smooth. Set a fine-mesh strainer in a bowl, and strain the blended mixture.

2. Press the pulp to extract all possible liquid, then discard the pulp. Pour your juice into your ice-pop molds, filling each three-quarter of the way.

3. Add in your ice pop sticks, then set to freeze for at least 5 hours or until solid. Serve.

Nutrition: Calories: 57; Carbs: 14.3g; Fat: 0.2g; Protein: 0.6g; Fiber: 1.1g

Melon Basil Moscow Mule Popsicles

Preparation time: 10 minutes + freezing time

Cooking time: 0 minutes

Servings: 10 popsicles

Ingredients:

- 1 lb. cantaloupe, peeled, seeded, & chopped
- 7 mint leaves
- 4 oz water
- 4 oz limeade
- 16 oz ginger beer
- 2 oz simple syrup

Directions:

1. Blend all the fixings into your blender until smooth. Set a fine-mesh strainer in a bowl, and strain the blended mixture.

2. Press the pulp to extract all possible liquid, then discard the pulp. Pour your juice into your ice-pop molds, filling each three-quarter of the way.

3. Add in your ice pop sticks, then set to freeze for at least 5 hours or until solid. Serve.

Nutrition: Calories: 42; Fat: 0g; Carbs: 10.8g; Protein: 0.1g; Fiber: 0.2g

Honeydew Mint Popsicles

Preparation time: 10 minutes + freezing time

Cooking time: 0 minutes

Servings: 10 popsicles

Ingredients:

- ½ honeydew melon, peeled, seeded & cubed
- 1/3 cup granulated stevia
- 10 mint leaves
- 1 tbsp lime juice
- 6 oz water

Directions:

1. Blend all the fixings into your blender until smooth. Set a fine-mesh strainer in a bowl, and strain the blended mixture.

2. Press the pulp to extract all possible liquid, then discard the pulp. Pour your juice into your ice-pop molds, filling each three-quarter of the way.

3. Add in your ice pop sticks, then set to freeze for at least 5 hours or until solid. Serve.

Nutrition: Calories: 35; Fat: 0g; Carbs: 9g; Protein: 0.1g; Fiber: 0.2g

Basil Watermelon Popsicles

Preparation time: 10 minutes + freezing time

Cooking time: 0 minutes

Servings: 12 popsicles

Ingredients:

- 1 lb. seedless watermelon, sliced
- 5 basil leaves
- 12 oz water
- 4 oz lime juice
- 1 oz honey

Directions:

1. Mix the honey plus water over medium heat. Allow the mixture to simmer, stirring until the honey melts. Let it cool.

2. Mix all the fixings in your large bowl, and pour your juice into your ice-pop molds, filling each three-quarter of the way.

3. Add in your ice pop sticks, then set to freeze for at least 5 hours or until solid. Serve.

Nutrition: Calories: 16; Carbs: 4.4g; Fat: 0g; Protein: 0.2g; Fiber: 0.14g

Orange Popsicles

Preparation time: 10 minutes + freezing time

Cooking time: 0 minutes

Servings: 12 popsicles

Ingredients:

- 3 cups orange juice
- 1 lime, juiced

Directions:

1. Mix all the fixings in your bowl until blended.

2. Pour your juice into your ice-pop molds, filling each three-quarter of the way.

3. Add in your ice pop sticks, then set to freeze for at least 5 hours or until solid. Serve.

Nutrition: Calories: 29g; Fat: 0.1g; Carbs: 6.8g; Protein: 0.4g; Fiber: 0.1g

Grapefruit Lemonade Popsicles

Preparation time: 10 minutes + freezing time

Cooking time: 0 minutes

Servings: 12 popsicles

Ingredients:

- 1/4 cup honey
- 2 ½ cups grapefruit juice
- 12 oz lemon juice
- 6 oz water

Directions:

1. Mix the honey plus water over medium heat. Allow the mixture to simmer, stirring until the honey melts. Let it cool.

2. Mix all the fixings in your large bowl, and pour your juice into your ice-pop molds, filling each three-quarter of the way.

3. Add in your ice pop sticks, then set to freeze for at least 5 hours or until solid. Serve.

Nutrition: Calories: 287; Fat: 2.5g; Carbs: 70g; Protein: 2.3g; Fiber: 1.5g

Lemon Granita

Preparation time: 5 minutes + freezing time

Cooking time: 5 minutes

Servings: 4

Ingredients:

- 3 lemons, juiced & zested
- 1/2 cup stevia
- 3 cups water

Directions:

1. Put the lemon juice plus zest in a small saucepan. Add the sugar, and boil over low heat. Simmer within 2 minutes, then remove and pour in the water.

2. Strain through your fine sieve, pour the mixture into an airtight container, and freeze for 2 hours.

3. Remove and mix with a fork to break the ice, then freeze for 1 more hour, repeating the same process twice.

Nutrition: Calories: 95; Fat: 0g; Carbs: 24g; Fiber: 0g; Protein: 0g

154

JUICE & TEAS

Watermelon Ginger Juice

Preparation time: 10 minutes

Cooking time: 0 minutes

Servings: 2

Ingredients:

- 4 cups seedless watermelon, cubed
- 1 tsp fresh ginger, peeled
- ½ tbsp fresh lime juice

Directions:

1. Blend all the fixings in your blender until smooth.

2. Through your fine mesh strainer, strain the juice and transfer it into your glasses. Serve immediately.

Nutrition: Calories: 95; Fat: 0.5g; Carbs: 23.5g; Protein: 1.3g; Fiber: 1.9g

Lemony Grapes Juice

Preparation time: 10 minutes

Cooking time: 0 minutes

Servings: 3

Ingredients:

- 4 cups Seedless white grapes
- 2 tbsp Fresh lemon juice

Directions:

1. Blend all the fixings in your blender until smooth.

2. Through your fine mesh strainer, strain the juice and transfer it into your glasses. Serve immediately.

Nutrition: Calories: 85; Fat: 0.5g; Carbs: 21.3g; Protein: 0.9g; Fiber: 1.1g

Cucumber Grapefruit Juice

Preparation time: 10 minutes

Cooking time: 0 minutes

Servings: 2

Ingredients:

- 4 seedless cucumbers, peeled & chopped
- 3 seedless grapefruits, peeled & sectioned
- 1 cup cold water

Directions:

1. Blend all the fixings in your blender until smooth.

2. Through your fine mesh strainer, strain the juice and transfer it into your glasses. Serve immediately.

Nutrition: Calories: 129; Fat: 0.7g; Carbs: 31.9g; Protein: 4.1g; Fiber: 3.1g

Kiwi Juice

Preparation time: 10 minutes

Cooking time: 0 minutes

Servings: 4

Ingredients:

- 4 medium kiwis, peeled & chopped
- 4 cups chilled filtered water

Directions:

1. Blend all the fixings in your blender until smooth.

2. Through your fine mesh strainer, strain the juice and transfer it into your large pitcher. Refrigerate to chill before serving.

Nutrition: Calories: 93; Fat: 0.8g; Carbs: 22.3g; Protein: 1.7g; Fiber: 3g

Zucchini Cucumber Juice

Preparation time: 10 minutes

Cooking time: 0 minutes

Servings: 1

Ingredients:

- 1 zucchini, peeled, seeded & sliced
- 2 cucumbers, peeled, seeded & sliced

Directions:

1. Blend all the fixings in your blender until smooth.

2. Through your fine mesh strainer, strain the juice and transfer it into your glass. Serve!

Nutrition: Calories: 35; Fat: 0.4g; Carbs: 5.7g; Protein: 0.5g; Fiber: 0.8g

Carrot Juice

Preparation time: 10 minutes

Cooking time: 0 minutes

Servings: 1

Ingredients:

- 5-6 carrots, peeled & chopped
- ¼ cup coconut water

Directions:

1. Blend all the fixings in your blender until smooth.

2. Through your fine mesh strainer, strain the juice and transfer it into your glass. Serve!

Nutrition: Calories: 50; Fat: 0.3g; Carbs: 11.5g; Protein: 1.2g; Fiber: 0.8g

Peach Cherry Juice

Preparation time: 10 minutes

Cooking time: 0 minutes

Servings: 2

Ingredients:

- ½ cup canned peach
- ½ cup canned cherry
- 1 cup water

Directions:

1. Blend all the fixings in your blender until smooth.

2. Through your fine mesh strainer, strain the juice and transfer it into your glasses. Serve!

Nutrition: Calories: 70; Fat: 0.1g; Carbs: 17.4g; Protein: 0.8g; Fiber: 1.5g

Celery Juice

Preparation time: 10 minutes

Cooking time: 0 minutes

Servings: 2

Ingredients:

- 8 celery stalks with leaves
- 2 tbsp fresh ginger, peeled
- 1 lemon, peeled
- ½ cup filtered water
- Pinch of salt

Directions:

1. Blend all the fixings in your blender until smooth.

2. Through your fine mesh strainer, strain the juice and transfer it into your large pitcher. Refrigerate to chill before serving.

Nutrition: Calories: 32; Fat: 0.5g; Carbs: 6.5g; Protein: 1g; Fiber: 2g

Lychee Juice

Preparation time: 10 minutes

Cooking time: 0 minutes

Servings: 2

Ingredients:

- 30 fresh lychees, peeled and pitted
- 1 cup of filtered water
- 2 tbsp simple syrup

Directions:

1. Blend all the fixings in your blender until smooth.

2. Through your fine mesh strainer, strain the juice and transfer it into your large pitcher. Refrigerate to chill before serving.

Nutrition: Calories: 159; Fat: 0.6g; Carbs: 40.6g; Protein: 1.2g; Fiber: 1.9g

Peach Juice

Preparation time: 10 minutes

Cooking time: 0 minutes

Servings: 2

Ingredients:

- 4 medium peaches, peeled, pitted & chopped
- 1 cup chilled water
- 1 tbsp fresh lime juice

Directions:

1. Blend all the fixings in your blender until smooth.

2. Through your fine mesh strainer, strain the juice and transfer it into your large pitcher. Refrigerate to chill before serving.

Nutrition: Calories: 119; Fat: 0.8g; Carbs: 28.1g; Protein: 2.8g; Fiber: 2.6g

Plum Juice

Preparation time: 10 minutes

Cooking time: 0 minutes

Servings: 2

Ingredients:

- 4 cups ripe plums, pitted and chopped
- 2 tbsp maple syrup
- 1 cup of filtered water

Directions:

1. Blend all the fixings in your blender until smooth.

2. Through your fine mesh strainer, strain the juice and transfer it into your large pitcher. Refrigerate to chill before serving.

Nutrition: Calories: 112; Fat: 0.4g; Carbs: 29.4g; Protein: 1g; Fiber: 1.8g

Mango Juice

Preparation time: 10 minutes

Cooking time: 0 minutes

Servings: 2

Ingredients:

- 4 cups mangoes, peeled, pitted & chopped
- 2 cups of filtered water

Directions:

1. Blend all the fixings in your blender until smooth.

2. Through your fine mesh strainer, strain the juice and transfer it into your large pitcher. Refrigerate to chill before serving.

Nutrition: Calories: 99; Fat: 0.6g; Carbs: 24.7g; Protein: 1.4g; Fiber: 2.6g

Lemony Black Tea

Preparation time: 10 minutes + steeping time

Cooking time: 0 minutes

Servings: 6

Ingredients:

- 1 tbsp black tea leaves
- 1 cinnamon stick
- 1 lemon, sliced thinly
- 6 cups boiling water

Directions:

1. Place the tea leaves, lemon slices, and cinnamon stick in a large teapot. Pour hot water over the ingredients and immediately cover the teapot.

2. Set aside for about 5 minutes to steep. Strain the tea in mugs and serve immediately.

Nutrition: Calories: 1; Fat: 0g; Carbs: 0.2g; Protein: 0g; Fiber: 0g

Warm Honey Green Tea

Preparation time: 10 minutes + steeping time

Cooking time: 15 minutes

Servings: 4

Ingredients:

- 4 lemon's peel, cut into strips
- 4 lemon slices
- 4 orange's peel, cut into strips
- 4 cups of water
- 4 green tea bags
- 2 tsp honey

Directions:

1. In a pan, add the strips and water. Let it boil, adjust to low heat, and simmer for 10 minutes. Take the strips out.

2. Add the tea bags, cover, and let it steep for 4-5 minutes. Discard the tea bags, and mix in honey. Serve with a slice of lemon.

Nutrition: Calories 16; Fat 0.2g; Carbs 5g; Protein 0.2g; Fiber 0.6g

Honey & Ginger Lemon Tea

Preparation time: 5 minutes

Cooking time: 5 minutes

Servings: 1

Ingredients:

- 2 to 3 tbsp lemon juice
- Hot water, as need
- Honey, to taste
- Fresh chopped ginger, to taste

Directions:

1. In a pan, add the water, and let it boil.

2. Add the rest of the fixings to your mug, pour the hot water, and stir well. Serve!

Nutrition: Calories 54; Fat 0.2g; Carbs 14g; Protein 0.2g; Fiber 0.2g

Peach Iced Tea

Preparation time: 10 minutes + steeping time

Cooking time: 5 minutes

Servings: 2

Ingredients:

- 2 earl grey tea bag
- 4 cups of ice
- 2 cups of water

For the Peach Syrup:

- 2 tbsp granulated stevia
- 1 ½ cups water
- 1 ½ cups diced peaches

Directions:

1. Steep the teas as per package instructions. Discard the tea bags, and keep them in the fridge for half an hour.

2. Add all the peach syrup fixings to a blender and pulse until chopped. Add to a pan, and simmer for 5 minutes. Strain into the tea mix well and serve.

Nutrition: Calories 51; Fat 1g; Carbs 13g; Protein 1g; Fiber 1g

Herbed Iced Tea

Preparation time: 10 minutes + steeping time

Cooking time: 0 minutes

Servings: 8

Ingredients:

- 6 cups boiling water
- 2 cups fresh herbs
- 8 tea bags
- 4 cups of clear juice

Directions:

1. Steep the tea bags in boiling water. Take the tea bags out, and add the remaining fixings.

2. Let it rest for 20 minutes. Strain well, and serve.

Nutrition: Calories 57; Fat 0.2g; Carbs 14g; Protein 0.1g; Fiber 1.2g

Lemon Ginger Detox Tea

Preparation time: 10 minutes + steeping time

Cooking time: 5 minutes

Servings: 2

Ingredients:

- ¼ tsp turmeric powder
- 2 cups water
- 1 (1 inch) of peeled ginger, sliced thinly
- ¼ tsp maple syrup
- 1 lemon, juiced
- Cayenne pepper, a pinch

Directions:

1. In a pan, add all the fixings, mix well, and let it boil.

2. Turn the heat off, and let it steep for 5 minutes. Strain and serve.

Nutrition: Calories 12; Fat 0.2g; Carbs 2.8g; Protein 0.3g; Fiber 0.6g

Melon Honey Green Tea

Preparation time: 10 minutes

Cooking time: 0 minutes

Servings: 2

Ingredients:

- 1 bottle of unsweetened Honey Green Tea (not sweet)
- 6 chunks of honeydew melon, seeded & cut into small squares
- 15 fresh mint leaves

Directions:

1. In your bowl, add all the fixings, and crush with a spoon.

2. Mix well, strain, and serve.

Nutrition: Calories 72; Fat 0.2g; Carbs 1.1g; Protein 0.1g; Fiber 1.1g

Iced Mint Green Tea

Preparation time: 10 minutes + steeping time

Cooking time: 0 minutes

Servings: 3

Ingredients:

- Fresh mint leaves, as needed
- 3 green tea bags
- 1 lemon, thinly sliced
- 2 cups of boiling water

Directions:

1. Steep the tea in boiling water, discard tea bags, and add to a pot.

2. Let it cool slightly, and add the lemon slices. Add your mint leaves, and let them rest for a few minutes. Serve.

Nutrition: Calories 0; Fat 0g; Carbs 0g; Protein 0g; Fiber 0g

Apple Iced tea

Preparation time: 10 minutes + steeping time

Cooking time: 0 minutes

Servings: 3

Ingredients:

- 4 cups of boiling water
- 1 lemon, thinly sliced
- 2 cinnamon sticks
- 4 cups of clear apple juice
- 2 English breakfast tea bags
- 1 red apple, peeled, cored & thinly sliced
- Honey, to taste

Directions:

1. Steep the tea bags in your boiling water for 15 minutes.

2. Discard the tea bags and add the rest of the ingredients. Chill in the fridge, and serve.

Nutrition: Calories 72; Fat 0.2g; Carbs 18.7g; Protein 0.1g; Fiber 1.2g

28-DAY MEAL PLAN

DAY	BREAKFAST	LUNCH	DINNER	SNACKS/ DESSERTS
1	Peach Banana Oatmeal	Pasta with Cheesy Tomato Sauce	Beef Skewers	Cinnamon Peaches & Apple
2	Ricotta Protein Pancakes	Chicken Lettuce Wraps	Shrimp Scampi Pizza	Fruity Jell-O Stars
3	Apple Cider Cinnamon Waffles	Lemony Scallops	Fiesta Chicken Tacos	Herby Cheese Biscuits
4	Spinach Egg Quiche	Shrimp & Tomato Bake	Grilled Salmon Steaks	Cinnamon Gelatin
5	Cheesy Chicken Spinach Frittata	Fried Rice with Kale	Herbed Salmon	Peach And Cream
6	Pear And Cornflakes Granola	Shrimp Lettuce Wraps	Gingered Turkey Meatballs	Peach Gelatin
7	Ricotta Pear Cream Bowl	Turkey Burgers	Asian Tofu Stir Fry	Baked Apricots with Honey
8	French Toast	Veggies and Apple with Orange Sauce	Lemony Salmon	Chocolate English Custard

9	Banana and Pear Pita Pockets	Tuna Stuffed Avocado	Rosemary Chicken	Rice Flakes Protein Bar
10	Breakfast Hash with Sausage & Spinach	Versatile Mac' n Cheese	Turkey with Rosemary	Plum & Nectarine Pudding
11	Potato Omelet	Roasted Beet Pasta with Kale and Pesto	Halibut Curry	Pear And Apple Crisps
12	Ripe Plantain Bran Muffins	Pasta with Asparagus	Chicken Cutlets	Rice Pudding
13	Breakfast Maple Cornflakes	Egg & Avocado Endive Wraps	Roasted Salmon and Asparagus	Egg Potato Bites
14	Melon Carrot Protein Porridge	European Beet Soup	Stuffed Zucchini Boats	Cranberry Kombucha Jell-O
15	Potato Hash with Egg Scramble	Greek Cucumber Salad	Mushroom Goulash with Rice	Beet Chips
16	Coconut Chia Seed Pudding	Beef & Spinach Burgers	Prawn & Vegetable Pasta	Apple Cider Muffins
17	Strawberry Cashew Chia Pudding	Pasta With Zucchini & Tomatoes	Brazilian Fish Stew	Potato Sticks

18	Pear Pancakes	Cucumber Tomato Salad	Chicken Salad Sandwiches	White Chocolate Pudding
19	Chicken & Zucchini Muffins	Beef & Mozzarella Burgers	Prawns with Asparagus	Cinnamon Pear Chips
20	Vanilla Crepes	Cheesy Chicken Meatballs	Mushroom Chicken Platter	Orange Popsicles
21	Feta Eggs in Tomato Sauce	Chicken & Apple Lettuce Wraps	Easiest Tuna Salad	Sweet Potato Chips with Avocado Smash
22	Peach Banana Oatmeal	Pasta with Cheesy Tomato Sauce	Beef Skewers	Basil Watermelon Popsicles
23	Ricotta Protein Pancakes	Chicken Lettuce Wraps	Shrimp Scampi Pizza	Vegetable Fritters
24	Apple Cider Cinnamon Waffles	Lemony Scallops	Fiesta Chicken Tacos	Honeydew Mint Popsicles
25	Spinach Egg Quiche	Shrimp & Tomato Bake	Grilled Salmon Steaks	Banana And Apricot Ice Cream
26	Cheesy Chicken Spinach Frittata	Fried Rice with Kale	Herbed Salmon	Cinnamon Peaches & Apple

27	Pear And Cornflakes Granola	Shrimp Lettuce Wraps	Gingered Turkey Meatballs	Fruity Jell-O Stars
28	Ricotta Pear Cream Bowl	Turkey Burgers	Asian Tofu Stir Fry	Herby Cheese Biscuits

COOKING CONVERSION CHART

Volume Equivalents (Dry)

US STANDARD	METRIC (APPROXIMATE)
⅛ teaspoon	0.5 mL
¼ teaspoon	1 mL
½ teaspoon	2 mL
¾ teaspoon	4 mL
1 teaspoon	5 mL
1 tablespoon	15 mL
¼ cup	59 mL
⅓ cup	79 mL
½ cup	118 mL
⅔ cup	156 mL
¾ cup	177 mL
1 cup	235 mL
2 cups or 1 pint	475 mL
3 cups	700 mL
4 cups or 1 quart	1 L
½ gallon	2 L
1 gallon	4 L

Volume Equivalents (Liquid)

US STANDARD	US STANDARD (OUNCES)	METRIC (APPROXIMATE)
2 tablespoons	1 fl. oz.	30 mL
¼ cup	2 fl. oz.	60 mL
½ cup	4 fl. oz.	120 mL
1 cup	8 fl. oz.	240 mL
1½ cups	12 fl. oz.	355 mL
2 cups or 1 pint	16 fl. oz.	475 mL
4 cups or 1 quart	32 fl. oz.	1 L
1 gallon	128 fl. oz.	4 L

Oven Temperatures

FAHRENHEIT (F)	CELSIUS (C) (APPROXIMATE)
250	120
300	150
325	165
350	180
375	190
400	200
425	220
450	230

Weight Equivalents

US STANDARD	METRIC (APPROXIMATE)
½ ounce	15 g
1 ounce	30 g
2 ounces	60 g
4 ounces	115 g
8 ounces	225 g
12 ounces	340 g
16 ounces or 1 pound	455 g